The Beginning and the End

Musings on a Journey Through Life

A Collection of Poems and Verse

Kenneth Moore

Honeybee Books

Published by Honeybee Books
Broadoak, Dorset
www.honeybeebooks.co.uk

Printed in the UK using paper from sustainable sources

ISBN: 978-1-910616-31-4

A CIP copy of this book is available from the Bristish Library

Front Cover Illustration: The 'Beginning and the End' by John Piper and Patrick Reyntiens photograph reproduced by kind permission of Stephen Cole.

Back Cover Illustration 'The Light of the World' by John Piper and Patrick Reyntiens photograph reprduced by kind permission of Robinson College, Cambridge.

By the same author -

From Fen to Mountain[2006]

To Edward Roy[Nobby]Clark
[1927 – 2014]

A great Art Master,motivator and friend.

'So this is your blue laundry phase then, Moore?'
'Yes sir.'
When shall we see your red phase? – Mm?'

This was in response to my attempt at producing a landscape painting of nearby laundry buildings as seen from the pottery and art room at Deacons Grammar School.

Preface

Born and brought up in an edge of Fens village [The Beginning] steeped in history and the witch hunts of more than 400 years ago that live on in folklore, our family lived close to my grandparents who were both true fenfolk born in villages close to the River Great Ouse in the Bedford Levels. Grandfather spoke little about his past as a young farmhand and then a farrier for a Mr Prior at a pleasantly named Meadow Farm, now sadly lost. The closeness of the whole family meant that I learnt a lot about many of my Great Aunts and Uncles. Visiting family and friends gave me the opportunity to appreciate and understand fenfolk and the harsh landscape they worked in and lived with. Great Uncle George and his commercial orchards were a revelation whilst the statutory visit in 'Sunday Best' to Great Aunt and Uncle Christmas's impressive fenland farmhouse left us in fear and trepidation even with the gift of a threepenny bit!

Grandfather as a farrier was called up to the Royal Field Artillery in the Great War and saw several years of action at Ypres and the Somme somehow surviving in body but doubtfully in mind, eventually joining the local village carrot and potato merchants, my father following in his foot - steps on demob from the RAF thus keeping farming in the family as it had been for so many generations. My grandparents then took up residence in the old Prince of Wales's Feathers [later named Lodge House] in the High Street opposite the quirky neighbours of White Hart pub and Methodist Chapel! Probably needing to release and express his deepest thoughts after the dreadful scenes he had witnessed in the Great War Grandfather became a Methodist Local Preacher pottering around the Fens to many isolated villages on his ancient, smoking motorcycle.

For myself time living in a city and later training in a professional career broadened horizons and with travel and sojourn across our glorious and richly endowed country and lands far, far away gave me time to ponder on my deepest and innermost thoughts and reminiscences, to the inevitable future [The End] and our passing from this world that we all must face.

Along the way I have been helped by Vaughan William's soothing and inspirational Fantasia on a Theme by Thomas Tallis, The Lark Ascending, Five Variations on Dives and Lazarus as well as George Butterworth's idyllic rhapsody 'A Shropshire Lad', his setting of Two English Idylls' and his last orchestral work – 'By the Banks of Green Willow', before he lost his life at 'the front' in 1916 at the Battle of the Somme. All truly intimate and pastoral English music.

Some 20 years or more were spent at a delightful Welsh longhouse caring for a friendly flock of motley sheep but now I reside in glorious Dorset with friendly Dorset country folk.

Kenneth Moore
Llanfynydd and Bridport 2014 and 2015

Contents

Preface

Fenborn, Spuds and Carrots 1

Grandma's Sunday Teas 2

A Winter's Tale 4

The Gift of Life and the Scourge of Death 5

The Witches of Wardibus 7

An Old Village Feast 8

Bygone Childhood Holidays 10

Fenland Summer Fruits 14

A Childhood Summer's Day 16

A Schoolboy's Saturday 18

Blackberries Upon Haddon Hill 20

A Young Chorister 22

The Midnight Service Organist 25

Repetoire of a Church Mouse 27

Clacton by Steam and Church Crawling 28

St.Margaret's and the Parish of Fletton 32

The Fens 35

Ramsey North Station 36

Thorney Strawberries and Honey 39

The Isle of Crowland 41

An Old Fenman 43

The Mad Cat 45

The Isle of Rams 46

A Country Poet 49

A Garden Privy 50

A London Suburban Traveller 51

Morocco and the Marrakech Express 56

Tuscany, Osterias and Sunflowers 58

Eboracum, Micklegate and No.19 60

Ratae Coritanorum and Greyfriars Richard 62

The White Lady 63

An Old Steam Engine 64

Francis and the 'Western' Sunset 65

Charlie and the Signal Box 68

Fred and Hairy Ned 70

An Old Welsh Longhouse 72

An Orphaned Lamb 74

The Heavenly Scilly Isles 75

The Quantocks and Kilve Shore 78

The 'Thankful Village' of Aisholt 80

The Tollers 81

Wraxall and Poet John Milton 82

Cattistock, GGS*, St. Peter and St. Paul 84

St. Nicholas'* Sanctity and Solemnity 86

The Capital of Marshwood Vale 87

The Dorset Asker 89

Dear Askerswell 90

The Bells of St. Mary's   91

Ancient Bridport and Burgages   92

Springtime in Deep Dorset Countryside   93

The Stilton Cheese and the Dorset Knob   95

Crossbones and Winchester Geese   97

Approaching Autumn   98

A Rural Church and God's Acre*   100

A Poor Church Mouse   102

The Light of the World   104

St. Andrew's, Woodwalton   105

The Beginning and the End   107

Acknowledgements   109

About the Author   110

About the Illustrators   111

Bibliography   112

Forthcoming titles   113

List of Illustrations

Charlie Sutton

The Gift of Life and the Scourge of Death
An Old Village Feast
Bygone Childhood Holidays
A Childhood Summer's Day
A Schoolboy's Saturday
A Young Chorister
Repetoire of a Church Mouse
The Fens
Ramsey North Station
The Isle of Crowland
An Old Fenman
The Mad Cat
The Isle of Rams
A London Suburban Traveller
Fred and Hairy Ned
The Quantocks and Kilve Shore
Wraxall and Poet John Milton
Springtime in Deep Dorset Countryside
Approaching Autumn
A Rural Church and God's Acre
A Poor Church Mouse
St. Andrew's, Woodwalton

Christopher Moore

Fenborn, Spuds and Carrots
Grandma's Sunday Teas
A Winter's Tale
The Witches of Wardibus
Fenland Summer Fruits
Blackberries Upon Haddon Hill
The Midnight Service Organist

Clacton by Steam and Church Crawling
St. Margaret's and the Parish of Fletton
Thorney Strawberries and Honey
A Country Poet
A Garden Privy
Morocco and the Marrakech Express
Tuscany, Osterias and Sunflowers
Eboracum, Micklegate and No.19
Ratae Coritanorum and Greyfriars Richard
The White Lady
An Old Steam Engine
Francis and the 'Western' Sunset
Charlie and the Signal Box
An Old Welsh Longhouse
An Orphaned Lamb
The Heavenly Scilly Isles
The 'Thankful Village' of Aisholt
The Tollers
Cattistock, GGS*, St. Peter and St. Paul
St. Nicholas* Sanctity and Solemnity
The Capital of Marshwood Vale
The Dorset Asker
Dear Askerswell
The Bells of St. Mary's
Ancient Bridport and Burgages
The Stilton Cheese and the Dorset Knob
Crossbones and Winchester Geese

The Beginning and the End
Musings on a Journey Through Life

Fenborn, Spuds and Carrots

I n the bleak and frozen fenland
   Some sixty years or more ago
   Midst frosty winds and ever deepening snow
A happening did occur so bland.
Few would notice, few would care.

Spuds and carrots were the norm
Dug from mud what'er the weather.
Weighed a ton, hardly a feather
As ducks flew over true to form.
Few would notice, few would care.

The humble carrot and the spud
Made 'kings' of many oh so far -
Warboys and Chatteris were on a par.
Brand and Rickwood won the mud!
Few would notice, few would care.

Dragged to school across the mud;
Father slid down slope to carrot wash
And ended up – what a splash!
All in the name of the carrot and the spud.
Few would notice, few would care.

Still young I reached the smoky city -
Central heating and warm bed linen,
Milk and bread to door, beginning
Life far more hectic – what a pity!
Village life missed, spuds, carrots and fair.
Few would notice, few would care.

Grandma's Sunday Teas

ate dictated City red and cream
Buses bumped along inhospitable droves that bad
Until just a few miles from our Fenland dream
Village of aged Grandma and Grandad
With some luck it met a green and cream
Omnibus under market clock – how glad
We were as numb hands were thumped
Against the bitter cold as we bumped
Into an old friend in the snow.
More like Siberia than Fens, I know.

But here is the country bus -
A welcome arrival but leisurely pace
Past village clock amidst the snow
Onto the thatched White Hart Inn.
Wrap up warm - it's freezing! Hope they're in
To welcome us with hot tea and
Glowing fire in the parlour grate.

What a wonderful house to stand
In that once sported the Prince of Wales'
Feathers as a tavern with haunted
Cellar, homely kitchen with vaulted
Chimney piece and black iron range,
Meat hooks from ceiling for the ham,
Oil clothed massive farm table with lashings of lamb,
And every goody one could wish for.
Cosy parlour and long table placed by door,
Burgundy velvet tassled cloth and
Crisp, white damask sheet set by hand
With pies, pickles, salads, cold meat and ham
Beside freshly made crisp buttered bread.

Follow this, if you can, by cake and ice cream,
Fruit and so many fizzy drinks – I shall scream
If I have any more. I must sit down
In weather beaten chair and frown
At the old shell case full of odds and ends

On the ancient mantelpiece sharing company
With brass candlesticks and many
Bits and pieces attached to coloured card.
Stuffed with festive fayre it is so hard
To cajole and squeeze into Sunday best
To walk across to chapel for a rest!

Gastronomic noises erupt in full
As on stiff pews the preacher's edict is so dull -
Fire, brimstone and hell is his shout
As right on cue his false teeth fall out
To land by a giggling aunt
In the front row ; from her sister a taunt
As all make to rise
To sing the final hymn - what a reprise!
As the aunt slinks from her seat -
Repent your sins , you're not complete!
No-one seems at all surprised but beam
As aunt is still bursting at the seam!
Children fidget anxious to leave
Pulling parents by the sleeve.
Attendance at evening service is an obligation
But surely not again until Rogation?
Next Sunday Grandad will be the local preacher.
Hop on motorbike as the holy teacher
Through Fen lanes and orchards to Over
Somersham and Cottenham but not quite Dover!
Fall in dyke and covered in frost and snow
He returns to Lodge House I know not how.

Now the time has come for us to leave
Upon the green and cream bus, I believe,
Back to civilisation in the city.
Village and chapel life we all miss
Mores' the pity!

A WINTERS TALE

No water for bathroom ablutions
Even blue tits must think of a solution
To break into milk through foil top
As horse and milk cart can never stop.

The Fens have never known such weather.
The year is now in April and no better
Days are foretold as horses struggle to hold
Carts from sliding into ditches as bold
Owners tie potato sacking to their feet
To stop a disaster on the ice sheet.
Water pipes still freeze as lagged in sack
Used for carrots and potatoes, people hack
At thick ice that covers everything.
As children we find it all so amusing.
In houses in the city the frost creates
Fancy patterns on windows and penetrates
Urban garden to leave as hard as iron;
Even chisels and crowbars are not fine
As Fen and urban workers strive to dig out
Vegetables that can be used and not rot.
Few potatoes, carrots and parsnips are saved
As once broken from home of ice and moved
To pits and shed they turn to mush
And what might have been food is now just slush!

Winter signs itself off with heavy snowfall,
Thunder and hailstones sized like a football!
Oh for a warm and joyful Spring day
After winter has lasted till the end of May!

THE GIFT OF LIFE AND SCOURGE OF DEATH

Jess the chestnut mare delivery horse
Demure and amiable on her daily course
    Around the city streets.
Fred gave her apple and carrot as a treat
Whilst Harry, the gardener collected steaming garden deposits
With ancient bucket and spade
That was truly golden and heaven made!
Jess plodded along the road
With her heavy load
And feed bag hung round her neck
To deliver the 'gift of life' every week –
Crispy white bloomer, crusty cob and iced fancies to the door
Something we would all adore!

Her fleet of foot friends were called to war
In fetid mud and screaming hell of Flander's fields
We cannot tell the fears
They felt in battle's heat
Many were called but few would return
And fell amidst the bloodied mire.
None would have a red poppy to mark where they fell
In the land of living and dying hell.
But what of Jess the delivery horse?
The worst!
Steaming nostrils and stamping feet in the bitter cold freezing,
winter air, Jess made her weary way back to the stable close to
gaudy and rowdy fair
To meet Joe, the friendly milk dray horse
To eat as much sweet hay as she was able.
Joe and Jess have no future in soft green meadow
With chiming churchyard bell.
It's just the bolt, the gun,the knacker's yard
And awesome hell!

THE WITCHES OF WARDIBUS

own by old mill pond now called the weir
Once was the ducking stool that put fear
Into those commonly labelled as a witch
Even though they had cats but no broomstick!
Four hundred years ago in sordid past of witch hunts
Awesome doings took place in village of Wardibus.
Ducking or swimming, to sink or swim
Was used to convict – but this was no win
As float you hung and sink you were drowned
Or pestered into confession not frowned
Upon by gullible physician and locals
Who gathered to witness, as crowd so vocal,
Arrest of hapless victims, half demented
Knowing the outcome their life be ended
By hanging from the neck at Quarter Session
For sorcery, sadism and satanic possession.
And so goes the tale of the 'witches' Samuel,
Victims of Throckmortons and Lady Cromwell.
Their names do not live on, just mockery
For all their supposed bewitching and sorcery
Remembered only as witches on broomsticks
To side of bus and football shirts 'The Witches'.

The village pond rests calmly in peace
With fish left over from the local feast.
Jo and Albert fishing from a wooden pier
Have great success hauling carp from the weir!

AN OLD VILLAGE FEAST

In the Fenland village it is Feast Week.
Most young boys with 'tanner' in hand seek
Out dodgem rides and then candyfloss
As Henry Thurston traction engines with brass,
Highly polished, and gold lettered canopy
Spew steam and smoke across whole panoply.
A haze of heat and steam engulf Main Street
As villagers try to gaze at the fleet
Of wagons and vehicles from upstairs windows
While generators roar and people do bellow
At the fun they have amidst coloured lights
That dim and brighten as machines fight
And struggle to cope with the load
As other vehicles vainly look for a road
To avoid traction engines and Feast traffic
And reach home with as little a panic.

Local brass band released from duty
At Rectory Gardens where tea and cake so fruity
Were made by goodly church ladies.
Musicians march past workers with their babies
Heading for Mr Bradley's fish and chip shop
Next to the Clock Tower – two pence for cod
And pennyworth of Fen potato chips in bag
As many labourers now light up a fag
And drink from a well earned pint of beer.
What's the time? It matters not – no fear
As the Feast goes into early hours of morning
When most are fit to drop and many yawning
And have spent most of their season's cash.
They have no holiday – this is their annual 'bash'.
Back to work next week if they can find
Their way home – a monotonous and hard grind.
Some 'worse for wear' are propped against

The doors of Village Clock – no haste!

Even the Village Clock is hard to see
Once critically acclaimed by Arthur Mee.
Shrouded in heat, steam and mystery
Just like roots of Fairs granted by Royalty
For all folk from country and town to enjoy
Whether they be yeoman, peasant or boy
Be it Gooseberry, Bridge or Fair for sheep and beasts
Blessed be they – long live Festivals and Feasts!

BYGONE CHILDHOOD HOLIDAYS

The old brown case bursts at the seams.
Father checks the door is firmly shut
Whilst mother makes sure we are all in order.
Gathered on the bright red
Eastern Counties bus conveying it's passengers
To the grimy, soot laden station
Bustling with porters and
Weary, dishevelled travellers looking
Vainly for the train to take them onward
To who knows where.

Filthy, dirty, greasy, hissing engine and
Grimy woebegone maroon coaches greet us.
Boarding the steam wreathed coaches
Children jostle to find an empty
Compartment and clean window
To watch the world go by.
Propelled by a forceful, dirty engine
Through countryside with dairy milk cows,
Frantically entering tunnels
With billows of smoke and surfacing
The other end into the sunlit sky;
Soot covered clothes and smuts in
The eye that causes a child to cry.

With screech of brakes and banging of doors
The vast and noisy terminus is reached.
Children and baggage gathered up
Mayhem is resumed as the family
Descend to the 'tube' in the bowels of
The earth to be transported at
Brake neck speed on dirty, red,
Rattling and whining trains bound for
Suburbia at Ruislip Gardens, Harrow and Moor Park.

Rising from below ground
Into the splendid 'palace of steam' -
Chocolate and cream carriages with

Shiny brass trimmed engines simmering
Under the huge platform clock
With clouds of smoke and steam
The train bound for West Country summer sun
Leaves the cavernous and echoing terminus;

Clatters on past houses, factories and
Iron foundries covered in thick grime;
Over rivers and canals with barges
Drawn by weary horses as the express
Engine shows off to sad, lone engines
Shunting rows of wagons in a yard,
Whistles at dirty slow suburban trains
And slows to pay homage to it's sisters and
Brothers lined up as fallen beasts of
The iron road at the engine rest home.

On past farmsteads, small town and village
Stations and chocolate factory, through
Tunnels, beside tree lined parks and
Glorious Georgian city with it's river weir
Glistening in the golden afternoon sun.
The steaming and hissing brass
Trimmed wonder of the iron road
Resplendent with nameplate over
Wheel arch simmers at temporary rest for
A well earned drink of water guided
Into her tanks by the young fireman
So proud of the job he performs to
Perfection under the towering roof
Of the 'temple of steam'.

Passing a grubby little pannier tank duly
Shunting her wagons and mail vans in the bay
It is little time before junctions for
Cheddar and Clevedon are passed
Where large cheeses are hand laden
Onto waiting railway vans for enjoyment
In the far reaches of the land.
On past a tiny halt where sand buckets
Are brim full with bright summer flowers.

Children wonder and are amazed at the
Views as they are propelled into a
Station bedecked with flowers in
Baskets hanging everywhere from the roof.
The button holed Station Master
Greets all his newcomers to seaside summer sun

Push chaired down sand strewn streets
Past brightly painted bay windowed
Guest house and hotels;
Claremont, Blenheim and Sea View
All display their 'no vacancy' signs and
Await their guests to return for tea.

Long terraces of holiday fun shops
Display every possible bucket and spade.
The pier train greets us
For a summer journey of joy and
Beach ready youngsters queue for
Their long awaited donkey ride.
Some sit squat on the sand
Watching Mr Plod make his arrest in a
Gaily decorated Punch and Judy show.

Parents and grandparents take it easy
Jealously guarding their favourite spot
On brightly coloured canvas deckchairs.
Uncle covers his shiny bald pate
From the searing sun and on shore breeze
With his much prized and
Very keenly read daily newspaper.
Oh dear, Uncle has accidentally knocked
Down a child's much admired sandcastle!

Not all is lost as children are marched
To the Regent Road floral clock
'If you wait Mr Cuckoo will at
Half past the hour come out of his chalet
On the very top of the clock.
There he is – what fun!'

Back to the beach for some more
Excitement on the donkeys and pony carriages.
Time goes so fast at the seaside.
Hurry up – it's nearly teatime at the B & B!
What will it be tonight?
Baked beans, bacon, sausages and tomatoes?

The sun sets, the day is at an end.
Parents stroll to the seafront
To see the illuminations and is that
Flat Holme lighthouse winking at us?
Tired little ones, cared for by grandparents, are tucked into bed
Ready for more fun and joy the next day!

FENLAND SUMMER FRUITS

Bikes oiled and checked,
Oilskin capes and leggings packed
In the old leather saddle bag.
Wipe the trusty machines with an oily rag
And collect the battered old
Peck fruit basket from the shed.
Wave goodbye and set off on
Annual journey from the city upon
The summer fruit picking and
Collecting deep in Fenland
From Great Uncle George's orchard.

Across unending flat Fen fields
And arrow straight diked roads
That will be hard with full loads
On our later return.
A glass of orange squash and
Cup of life giving tea - what a treat
That refreshes in mid August muggy heat
At Grandma's cool Lodge House.

We've sat too long and pedal madly
Onto thoughts of orchards bursting grandly
With the good fruits of the land
To cram frantically into mouths and
Make baskets brim full.
As extra fruit is loaded on panniers
Watch out! Those wasps have no manners!
Leave the fount of all fruits oh so full
In high spirits to mull
Over a successful journey so far.
More drinks – Grandma you're a star!

Offload armfuls of ripe fruit and
Balance loaded peck basket by hand
On the old dicky seat of the crossbar.
Blackening sky and billowing clouds

Signal stair rod rain afar
As the precious load weighs down
On the unending flat roads a car
Speeds by to reach it's goal thrown down.

Bikes and bodies creak and groan
As stair rods and gale winds do moan
And batter game players more akin
To drowned rats with no oilskin.
Till, too late, we steam
As journey ends with streams
Of water pouring down.
Oh so good to be back in town.
The priceless cargo from afar
Is prepared for jam and kilner jar.
The journey over for another year;
More miles again
For fruit to bear.

A CHILDHOOD SUMMERS DAY

School is finished – what a shame!
Let's run amok and play a game
Of hide and seek and bat and ball.
Mind the paving slab lest you fall -
Grazed knees and arms it doesn't matter!
There's a big puddle let's have a splatter!
Wet clothes, wet shoes, go to mother
For a change into something or other.

The sun is shining – no it's not!
Big black thunderclouds - we'll get the lot!
Lightning and thunder make us scream
As water pours down the street as a stream.
The rain has stopped, the air is heavy,
Street workmen lean on tools to have a bevy.
Race you down to the end of the street
To the old allotment – a great place to meet.

Hissing steam engines go rushing past.
They seem to be going awfully fast.
An old freight train chugs along -
It would take an age to join the throng.
Jubilee, 9F, B1 and Mallard, the 'streak'
All pass as the timetable reaches it's peak.
Barrels of honey at Farrow's factory gate
Await their collection and onward fate.
Coal wagons a plenty in the goods yard;
But the day is coming to an end and it's hard
To leave for tea from our meeting place.
We'll need to wash grime from the face
As another storm builds dark in the sky.
To chums we wave – goodbye, goodbye!

Scrubbed clean and tea on the plate;
Father is running somewhat late -

Bike in the shed, clips off, join us at table
As we try to tell as much as we are able
Of the first day of summer hols
When we all needed the use of brols!
Many more summer days to come
To join with chums and have such fun!

A SCHOOLBOY'S SATURDAY

T is dark and cold, plain damp and wet.
I rise from bed sleepy, but yet
Breakfast is consumed so fast.
I'm on my bike and cycle past
The still sleeping people
In the city beneath the steeple.

My lamp picks out the road
I must enter if I am to load
Fruit and veg aboard the trailer
Bound from Priestgate's border
To the city market in order
To sell to people passing through.
Bananas, apples – would anyone like a brew?
The sweet scent of fruit is overpowering
As I am released by owner Mr Bowring.

To wend my way back home.
More breakfast and toast to come
Then I bike to watch the trains go by
New England Depot and River Lane - my
What excitement - the Fair Meadow
And Cripple Lane all allow
Avid trainspotters a paradise and feast.
How I wish for a footplate ride treat
From East to North Stations as a pilot
On old 4F, B1 or tank engine – oh what
Joy unconfined to report to chums!

Once more at light fall I am told
At the market to reload unsold
Fruit and veg to be taken to store
At Priestgate where I am paid more
As Mr Bowring has had a good day.
Feeling bountiful with so much to say
I pedal through the city with lamp aglowing
Past the football ground still buzzing
Long after the match has ended.
What team were slain but valiantly defended?
Frickley Athletic or could it be Spennymoor?
Results are on the Sorts Report – four
Goals for our star striker and Posh
Won by nine clear goals – gosh
What a score as hot buttered crumpets
Laid on plates, are just left as bits.
Would you like some orange fizzy drink?
Of course – I don't even have to think!

Round to Wade's, the cycle shop,
To collect the Pink 'Un paper – and stop !
He has some stamps I must acquire
For my collection to which I aspire
With my hard earned cash.
Home to read how Posh came to squash
Poor Spennymoor up the creek
Better luck to them next week!

BLACKBERRIES UPON HADDON HILL

'Tis the season of bountiful fruitfulness
As blackberries ripen and are at their best
Before flies and wasps do devour
And give you a big surprise in the bower
Or hedgerow across country field!
Best to pick now for a stupendous yield
That are set aside for jam or kilner jar
And join other preserves collected from afar
Stored in neat ranks on shelves in pantry.
But wait! We're running short of blackberry!
Cast iron gloves, hand hoe and bikes to fore
As we pedal into countryside for more
To fill jars and pots to overflowing
And ready for the stiff winter forthcoming!

Across the Ermine Street we warily tread
To uncharted lanes and fields ahead
Beneath the superb eminence of Haddon Hill
Complete with television masts still
Beaming out their red warning lights astride
The rolling Huntingdonshire countryside.

Small village of Morbone set in green pasture
With old farm and church a little further
Is blissful peace and solitude to savour
As we head up track, the blackberry arbour
That crosses fields to the church at Haddon -
Dear little building much of which is Norman,
Eyes are diverted to brambles with berries -
They will go with many jams and chutneys.
Hand hoes hook the laden brambles down
As we all 'muck in' and 'go to town'
On juicy blackberries by the score -
Sadly many in rush fall to floor!
Stained hands, stained gloves - what a mess
As our gathering skills are put to the test.

Suddenly a shout rings out from far away.
We stop our gleaning and promptly stray
To nearby five bar gate and find
Gentleman with gun and dog behind
Waving frantically for us to leave
Or else our bottoms will be like a sieve!
We gather up tools, blackberries and bikes
And head off down lane to safely hike
To Haddon village and church's safety
As long as we don't disturb peace and sanctity!
We walk sedately down garlanded bower
To the dear church set amidst the flowers.
Thankfully we do not need church's sanctuary
As gentleman did not threaten our hard won safety.

We leave the peace and quiet of Haddon village
With mountains of blackberries from the pillage
Of the hedgerows near Haddon and Morbone
And take home to pantry what's almost a stone!
Stained and scratched across our arms
We check the maps to see which farms
The gentleman with gun and dog came from.
But it matters little now you see
As blackberries are safely in the cool pantry!

A YOUNG CHORISTER

A dark, deep winter's day.
Bicycle propped against the old church tower.
People huddled in great coats and scarves
Rush past in the lantern lit alleyway
Twixt church and the old corn exchange.

Into the warm glow of the ancient church
Lit by the warm tungsten lamps and
The Christmas lights adorning the
Tree set in the North Aisle by the font.
Gowned up in crimson red and white
Cassocks with stiff starched neck frills
That must surely restrict our sweet voices.

As Master of Music and organist
Flies by in gown as a ship in full sail to
Pass music making today to the
Young organ scholar who nervously
Tickles the ivories on the great organ.
Practice of the Festival of Nine Lessons
And Carols begins hesitantly
As the Master waves his baton madly in the
Air like a demented fairy's wand!
Occasional irate tapping on a
Choir stall wakes up a dozing chorister
And a Third Former aims a chewing gum
Pellet down the line of choristers scoring
A direct hit on the Chemistry Master in
Full flow of his heavy, laboured bass
Singing of a most favoured carol.
A caustic glare is conveyed to all;
Nothing more is said or needed!

Has my voice broken for the descant
Sung only a week ago with gusto and
What of my great pal, Bloggs?
Would his voice be crystal clear and

Tone perfect at the most critical moment of
The solo of 'Once in Royal David's City'?
All is well, at least until next week!

Cassocks hung on respective hooks as
Choristers leave to the Master of Music's
Rendition of heart warming Christmas carols.
Into the frozen late afternoon
Along ill lit streets past fishmonger's stalls
Washed down to leave sheets of gleaming ice.

People rush by huddled against the cold.
Market traders frozen to the marrow
Stack fruit and vegetables by the Guildhall.
The West Front and spires of the Cathedral
Lit eerily blood red with winter's
Setting sun behind Minster Precinct gateway. Shopkeepers
close up premises against
Forthcoming hard frost and intruders.

Liptons store below the imposing
Town Hall remains open against all odds.
A large piece of Cheddar Cheese, with rind, of course,
Placed in large paper bag is collected by
The chorister who, with bike, and satchel on crossbar,
Heads south of the city closing for the night
To home beneath towering chimneys that
Spew clouds of dark sulphurous filth
Into the almost blood red sky.
Frozen coat and gloves of a chorister,
Still humming the carols just sung,
Are hung in the hallway.
Home to a warm house and food -
Stew and dumplings, no doubt!

THE MIDNIGHT SERVICE ORGANIST

S tars shine bright in moonlit sky.
Snow flurries fall as white confetti
Gently covering paths and roofs.
Tis the magic hour before Christmas Day.
The organist is wrapped in warm blanket
Beside a roaring log fire.
She's determined to stay!

A young self - taught organist is called away
To lead the Midnight Service
On this most special of nights.
Press the green button from the organ loft
To start the hissing and whirring
Of the great piped machine and bellows.
Watch the tiny lead weight drop to tell
All is ready to make music.
So many manuals of ivory keys,
Ranks of stops and large and small pedals
Make the machine an awesome beast
Of untamed power and wind.

No-one has yet come to be blessed or be
Inspired by the organist's repertoire.
Time for soft music with
Subtle improvisation and modulation -
Bach's masterful organ choral prelude
'Leibster Jesu wir sind hier'- ' Dear Jesus
We are here' an appropriate choice for all
Gathered to hear the minister's welcome
And partake of the Holy Communion.

This stirring carol should keep them awake -
'O Come All Ye Faithful
Joyful and Triumphant' and then
Something a little softer and quieter -
'O Little Town of Bethlehem' before
Holy Communion, the most reverent part

Accompanied by a soft, contemplative organ
Choral prelude - 'Nun komm der heiden heiland.'
The minister seems to approve as he
Nods – or is he falling asleep?
Time to wake them up again and deliver them from
Over indulgence in communion wine.
'Hark the herald angels sing
Glory to the new born King'.
Come along, sing with gusto,
Sing with all your heart -
Christmas Day is almost here!
The organ is doing all it can with
All sound and skill available.

Music in this magic hour lifts the
Organist's spirit for his finale!
As participants walk out
Into the crystal clear star studded
Christmas morning the organist gives
All in his power for a full blown rendition of
Bach's Toccata and Fugue in D Minor.
Ivories, pedals, stops and loft rattle;
Bellows plead for an easier time to come.

All you good people kept from warm beds
Have celebrated and sung in
The birth of your great Saviour.
Joy, peace and goodwill this festive tide.
Well done good and faithful organist.
Happy Christmas to all!

REPETOIRE OF A CHURCH MOUSE

T is a balmy summer's day
   As church mice come out, the organ to play
   In and out of the pipes they go
The music they make is discordant
But no worse than organist Mrs Mount
Who falls asleep all the time
Only to be woken by church bell chime
As daddy mouse conducts with candle taper
Chorus of young mice with music papers
Propped against old hymnal books
As candles drip wax into so many nooks.
The young mice sing out their souls
But don't look that fine
As they've been at the communion wine!
Mrs Mount sleeps and snores in her shawl
The Vicar has nodded off in the stall!
What of participants?
There are none at all!

CLACTON BY STEAM AND CHURCH CRAWLING

Gather up bikes and accoutrements
And wheel into guard's van of train
Arrived behind dirty, hissing steam engine
At bedraggled, woebegone East Station;
Ready to leave for seaside in few moments
Across flat fenland, mile after mile
Until City of Cambridge is duly reached
Where our steam engine's thirst is quenched
Before we head for unknown rural halts.

My school friend with my parents is at ease
As train moves onward through pleasant
Countryside of Essex and Suffolk villages
Past church, manor house and many a cottage.
Light puffs of white smoke do much to please
As we venture deeper into rural Anglia
Pausing at dear wayside halts and stations
Of Shudy Camps, Wixoe, Clare and Cavendish
And country town of Haverhill at least.

The journey, along lines later axed by Dr. Beeching
Is a pleasure untold as we watch the
Odd milk churn and basket of racing pigeons
Loaded and unloaded from our steam train
As signalman hands token to driver passing
And we wave to farmer on tractor at handgate
Waiting to cross with his herd of cows
Returning from milking at nearby dairy.
The end of journey to Clacton is nearing.

The countryside, once wooded valley of the Stour
Now becomes flatter, sandier heathland.
From town of Colchester to beckoning sea
At Clacton and retirement enclave of Frinton
Past Alresford, Weeley and Great Clacton by four

Our steam train clanks into Clacton terminus.
The end of the line has been reached -
Bikes are collected from the guards van
As we gird ourselves to pedal to the shore!

A verandahed holiday bungalow awaits our coming
And we sit down to consume orange lemonade
To quench our thirst from long journey
And read up on the local churches around.
With country bike rides that are forthcoming
Load films in cameras and check notebooks.
Then pack ready haversacks with all that's needed.
All prepared and evening meal 'demolished'
We 'hit the sack' early for what we'll be doing.

Head out of town past gaily painted seaside shops
To call at St. James of Little Clacton
Where we admire and photo timbered belfry
Before we pass down delightful village street
And by the Queen's Head pub before our next stop.
Out on the open road we pedal madly
Ahead of impending August storm and thunder
And reach our next call without a soaking.
Across Weeley Heath – is it raining? No it's not!

St.Andrew at Weeley has a fine brick tower
So we stop for lunch by churchyard gate and devour
Sandwiches, apples and packets of crisps
Whilst consulting maps for next part of trip.
We head out once more from the wonderful bower
Of Weeley's church and nearby Guttridge Hall.
Out across countryside amid balmy air,
Through Thorpe Green and Beaumont com Moze
Until Great Oakley is reached amongst the flowers.
What a delight to be at All Saints in favoured company –
A truly rural churchyard
With no signs of shears or dreaded mower
As birds, bees and butterflies fly all around
And crows and rooks make raucous cacophony
About a vernacular weatherboarded tower
Complete with pyramidal roof and weather vain.

Time doth not wait as we head down country lane
For well earned tea and break that's in our mind!

* * * * * * * * * * * *

Next day comes as break from' country church crawling'.
We visit secondhand bookshops
Cramped to overflowing
Whilst avoiding seaside and novelty emporium
That abound at every corner of the town
Selling all from beach balls to everything
Avid beach enthusiasts might crave for.
Young children with parents in tow
Invade shops for the latest in sunglasses,
Swim caps, goggles and fins – in fact anything!

Weighed down by vols. on churches
Of Essex, be they by Pevsner orMee,
They're just what we need
And will keep us enthralled
In an encapsulating read!
Sadly not for free,
But certainly a must!
Plenty of scope to travel the byways
As we cycle once more
Into verdant countryside to seek out
Solemn and peaceful churches – for us a first!

Sadly our holiday is coming to an end
But not before time is wisely spent
Pedalling abroad to look down on St.Osyth Priory beside
Blackwater
Near Great Bentley, just round next bend.

What a village green to behold – It must the size of a common
or at least fourfold!
With St. Mary the Virgin as guardian mater.
On through Hare Green to reach St. George's
At Great Bromley, a fine rural church to attend.

A proud and compact East Anglian style
With big West tower and hammerbeam roof
To nave of such superb magnificence!
Then take life in hands to cross Norwich road
Past dear thatched lodge near Bentley Hall pile
Into Little Bentley village to parish church
With delightful tower and embattled brick porch.
We push on with little time left to pass
Tendring Heath and Goose Green within few miles.

Much like Great Oakley is the village of Tendring
With parish church of St.Edmund, King and Martyr -
A charming place of worship, rest and peace
With dear old timber porch amongst such a
Natural God's Acre of waist high grasses
waving
In the thundery August time air.
Sadly it's time to leave secluded Tendring
To return once more for the final time
To Clacton for tea just as sun is setting.

Ancient timber porch

Essex 'church crawling' finished for anoth-
er year
We collect together all our gear and be-
longings -
Cameras, notebooks and not forgetting
All those volumes bought from bookshops.
What a find!
Bikes are wheeled down road loaded so high!
My parents in tow with bags some way behind.
Our train is steaming gently at plaform 5
As guard helps to load bikes aboard – no fretting.
We're off home but there are no tears!

We have been witness to English village life over so many
years
With simple, rural churches in peaceful, verdant setting.

ST.MARGARET'S AND THE PARISH OF FLETTON

S t.Margaret's stands as a cross to bear
True testimony and witness
As haven of peace and quiet away from stress
Of roaring city oh so near.
Set amidst spreading cedar and
ancient trees
Next to solemn gardens of Georgian rectory
Where tea and cucumber sandwiches are often served
By rector and wife to selected company.
If selected it's best to call as you are so revered!
Outside the churchyard gate lies a bland High Street
That doth follow course of ancient Fleet.
Lines of manicured Victorian terraced houses
And then the rundown Coach and Horses
Set next to baronial Magistrate's Court
          With library and bank both 60's afterthought.
We leave St.Margaret's cool depths of solemnity –
My friend prefers more Catholic hierarchy
With many candles and incense for burning
And finds the organ does need tuning!
In energy sapping humid August air
A call is made at ancient bakery for fresh baked fare
Only to meet Mr Chapman, the baker, white as a ghost,
Covered in flour from his labours as 'host'
To his glorious Farmhouse bread.
Past Wick's Fish and Chips – what a spread!
And then beyond Goods Yard with heaps of coal
As brickyard chimneys spew out their filth – they have no soul!
Not like Jack Scotting whose little shop
          We pass – his whistling still continues non stop
Even though he's long since passed on

Across the road from grim Board School upon
The hill encaged in iron railings – what a reminder!
We part and go our separate ways.
For tea - fresh farmhouse bread with layers of butter!
Happy teenage days!

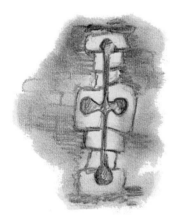

'Squint' inside St. Margarets

THE FENS

*T*he Fens is a 'feeling' conditioned, you see,
By the smell of it's earth as tangy as salt air of the sea.
Our childbirth, childhood and family life
Lead onto traditions and work, not strife.
The Fens seem so primeaval and harsh
As silence is broken across the marsh
By caw of pheasant and whirr of geese
As they seek more for their next feast.

At night the silence grows eerily
As a new moon glides gracefully by
Across the sky reflected as a glow
In the perfectly still waters of Fen below.
And yet in cloudless blue skies in spring
The skylark flies high on the wing
And sings it's heart out as it soars
Over fields of wheat and barley, stores
Of harvest yet to be gleaned
Followed soon by a sight often feared
Of stubble fires raging madly
With billowing plumes of smoke sadly
Blacking out the sun as if evening had come
Inexorably across bleak flat land and home.
A ritualistic finale to an idle hot summer
Heralding tired, short days of autumn and winter.
'Hills are alright but it's a good sky wasted.'
So said the old Fenman as he rested.

RAMSEY NORTH STATION

Oh to be in Ramsey North when the train is there!
Like as not you might as well be anywhere -
Black Bank, Smeeth Road and Six Mile Bottom
Along with Shippea Hill are all forgotten
Lost amidst the never ending Fen.
Not even Beeching wrote their name with pen -
All gone to railway heaven in the sky
Just like Ramsey East and North termini!
Where did you wish to travel to on this line?
Somersham ,Cambridge or Holme Fen – that's fine
But just be sure you are well on time
As there's only one train a week on this Northern line!

Crossing through jet black Fen soils
The grubby J6 of New England depot toils
With just two wagons and an old brake van
Puffing steam from stove pipe and billycan
As the guard prepares to produce the tea
For him and crew as they approach the 'sea';
And 'sea' it may well have been many a year
Ago as they edge past the Whittlesey Mere.
Not long to go to Ramsey North for a break
When they can have a mug of tea and slice of cake
Gratefully received from the fireman's wife
As she knew this job was so full of strife!

The train arrives and shunts it's wagon.
Driver and fireman fancy a pint at 'The Flagon'
Public House close by the yard
But know this would be wrong – it's so hard
To drive the train back up the line
And pick up beet and spuds - but they'll be fine.
The cake and tea go down a treat.
Driver, fireman and guard back on feet
Prepare for journey back across Fens

But not before they've loaded up hens
Left by that Mr Swannell, you know
To be dropped at the halt of Ramsey Hollow.

The train sets off tender first
As at the North there is no turntable,
Past New Fen and Ugg Mere as fast as able
But stops at Nightingale's Corner to quench it's thirst
By means of rope and bucket into dyke.
Fireman sits astride boiler with rod in water tank
To try to catch infernal stickleback!
This journey would be faster by far by bike!

Farmhands load beet, carrots and spuds
Into coal wagons now covered in mud.
Last call is at Decoy before the main line.
Driver, guard and fireman are doing fine
As the little train reaches Holme Crossing.
Now let's get back home to depot – no fussing.
The precious Fen load is put to bed
And the J6 kindly watered and fed.
All over for another week to North Ramsey;
Crew and engine can now take it easy!

THORNEY STRAWBERRIES AND HONEY

'The flower it is of many a fair tree'
That be true of Thorney Isle so free
And fair haven of orchards, bowers and abbey
Which still bears some resemblance, maybe,
Of peaceful, monastic and rural bliss
Once village and abbey have a blessed bypass!
To the North lay vast Bedford Level Fenland
Across Old Pepper Lake and Singlesole from Crowland.

But one humid, thundery August day
With noisy traffic far. far away
I spied an ancient cottage set below the road
Alongside an arrow straight Fenland loade.
Rows of strawberries I then saw
Set in jet black soil with a bed of straw.
A rugged gentleman stood at tarred barn door
With, if I was not mistaken, a twin bore
Shotgun slung under his arm!

But I'm sure he really meant no harm!
Earl Grey tea, cream and strawberry jam scones later
We sat in his parlour and had a good natter
Of fenland life and his beloved honey
Sold to Thorney tearooms for plenty of money.
Showing me his pride and joy – hives, home of the bee
I never asked his name nor would he tell me.
So we parted company and I gave him thanks
For gifts of strawberries and honey in packs
Loaded with care onto my pannier.
And headed off to the village in a gentle manner.

The Abbey bell tolled to tell the end of day.
At the Abbey tearooms, now closed, I pay
Attention to a brightly coloured sign
In window – 'local honey for sale' –that's fine

As I had already consumed much for free!
But would there be honey still for tea?
Of course, plenty for both thee and me.
I leave this most ancient Isle of the Fen
Pedalling into the sunset – I'll be back again!

THE ISLE OF CROWLAND

Few think of Crowland as of any consequence
    Just another Fen Isle worth but a few pence!
    But village and Abbey stand sentinel as days gone by -
Haven for monk and traveller in the marshy
Land full of wildfowl and fish -
A poacher's paradise to place on the dish!

From the Isle of Thorney , past Buke Horn and Powder Blue
Protected by 'witches broom' trees against the hue
Of a crimson and blue winter sky.
Across Cat's Water past Flood Farm by
Kennulph's Farm and the Old South Eau
To Abbey that stands as support to friend and foe.
At it's centre a unique bridge called Trinity -
A triangular edifice, as you may well see,
Beneath which sit old gentlemen, bent
With sticks, who act as the local parliament
Long since lost it's waterways that
Once ran beneath it's arches along with royalty but
Now more akin to a signal box with no station
But still keeping it's long tradition.

Invasions, earthquakes and floods a regular event,
The latest and worst being '47 when time was spent
At all costs to prevent loss of life and tell
Villagers of impending doom by the 'danger bell'.

In the Abbey where miracle of 'Reunited Earl' is told
To prove that Crowland is not boring even if cold
Waltheof's miracle makes the Abbey come alive
On a warm day as local bees head for the hive
Most probably of the gentleman at nearby Thorney
To make honey their endless and daily duty
Amidst ancient stones and waving grass
Of God's Acre The Abbey's past
Has crept up and lifted a burden
To remind one of monks garnering in garden

And orchard under the guiding shadows
Of St. Guthlac's Abbey and All Hallows.

The day is ended, the old gentlemen gone
From the triangular bridge, their throne.
Peace reigns abroad as bees buzz and hum.
The traveller must pedal into setting sun!

AN OLD FENMAN

On a morning bright, crisp and even
Sometime before the Feast of St. Stephen
A lone figure forlornly hoed the beet
In a field, no trees or hedges in sight.

By the old gate with no fence
Lay his rusty steed worth nothing but pence.
Dressed in greatcoat tied with twine
He struggled across field as wind did whine.
Bitterly cold and no doubt frozen to marrow
He leant old frame against hoe and barrow
Then bluntly spoke as Fenmen only do -
A languid drawl through and through -
'W'ere d'you come from?' or something.
Conversation with fen folk is almost nothing.
They are but to the point, stoical and stubborn.
A good talk with them you have to earn.

Having spun him a yarn about the beet
He uneasily shuffled to his feet,
Moved awkwardly to his rusty steed.
A greaseproof paper packet he then untied
And lowered himself to the ground
To eat his doorstep docky without a sound,
Propped up against the trusty bike
With greatcoat as shelter in spite
Of the accursed, perishing wind
That all wished they could leave behind.

Docky finished, greaseproof paper in pocket,
He mounted his old bike with hoe and bucket
And squeaked off slowly down the track
With not a word or a looking back.
Wind did moan and reeds did rustle

As he left for town not in a hustle
But smoothly squeaking his sole way home
To roaring fire, his castle, his throne.
To bed, to sleep, to peace, no pain
To start his day's journey all over again.

THE MAD CAT

The Mad Cat lies in the village of Pidley
Just down the road from Warboys in a tiddly.
You may well be tiddly as you leave the Mad Cat
If you've spent many hours or near that
With true Fen locals who can't agree
How to speak a few village names or three
Such as Magdalene, Bozeat and Farcet
'Wots it matter anyway how you sez it?'
The old gentleman rose from the settle
His weary frame needing a brew of the kettle
And headed off home – he had a point.
His friends under the sign had another pint
And raised their glasses to 'The Cat'.
Life's too short – we'll drink to that!

THE ISLE OF RAMS

nce a sylvan setting amidst noisome fen mire
The Isle of Rams was rich and the desire
Of many a nobleman, monk and squire;
A perfect haven for them as long as fire
Did not consume the richly endowed barns
Fed by much land, waterways and farms.
All was peace amidst marsh and fen
With many monks contemplating and hence
Writing and praying for lost souls and townsmen
Whilst Abbot and guests became so fat
On the bounteous harvest of the land that
They controlled until monastic sites
Were taken by Henry without a fight,
Handed to lords to use as they saw fit
With yeoman and peasants not given a bit!

Calm returned at Ramsey after all the sin
Until poor William Cromwell, Oliver's cousin,
Who had cloth for fine coat packaged
To his house by express mail carriage.
The London cloth came with the awful plague;
Before coat was finished all suffered fatigue
And William, his family and the tailor
Along with 400 Ramsey folk were given no favour
As all promptly fell ill and perished
And town and inhabitants all but vanished!

Now guardian to just Church and Abbey Gatehouse
With Church and Abbey Greens and pond in their place
To form a delightful rural setting
With old, ornate estate cottages bounding
Greens and pond like guardian angel,
Holding hands and keeping silent vigil!
The wide Great Whyte at centre of town

Reminds one of river that once was the crown
Of rich gardens and orchards of the Abbey where
Monks did labour and garner produce for Fair
That was held in Great Whyte with pomp and ceremony
To ensure the Abbey never went short of money.
Like Crowland, Thorney and Medehamstede*
Ramsey Abbey found plenteous food to feed
It's rich patrons and visiting Royalty
Who called regularly for no paltry
Feast oft taken at nearby Bodsey House,

The Abbot's retreat and summer residence.
The town folk were conveniently forgotten
As long as they did penance with their only oxen!

Little happens in Ramsey town today
With Abbey gone and only Church at which to pray.
The ancient sites of Bodsey and Worlick
Are bleak and cold enveloped by thick
Fenland mist on a once bright autumn day.
The old buildings no longer resound, nay
Jangle and laugh at the Abbot's high table
But remain ghostly remnants by the stables
Of days gone by when all made merry
And toasted the Abbot and monks with sherry!

*Medehamstede was Peterborough Abbey

A COUNTRY POET

N either Fenland nor Peasant poet
Rather one of heaths, commons and woodlands that
Abounded around his home in village of Helpston
Centre of the kingdom's largest Roman occupation.
In age of discovery and desire to understand,
An exciting time underground and over ground
For such a talented, gifted and intelligent man
John Clare revelled in the delicate land
That unfolded by riverside, heath and village alike
His walks by wandering, lugubrious pike
Laden Nene, through water meadow, by mill pond,
Flower bedecked heath and sweet, luscious woodland.
Past cottages, farmhouses, churches and hamlet,
Walcot Hall, Woodcroft Castle and the Hall at Pellett,
Southey Wood, Ladywood and Sutton Heath -
All were 'his country' honoured beneath
His feet as he heard the distant calling bell
Beckoning the faithful few away from 'hell'
To salvation and a sense of truly belonging.
Times were then when he went lazily wandering
Richly endowed hedgerowed lanes
Until time came for him to be lain
Down below the parish church clock
At mid-day his own lines come flood-
ing back...
 'The mid-day hour of twelve the clock
counts 'oer'
The day is near over – a
sultry stillness lulls the
air.

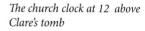

*The church clock at 12 above
Clare's tomb*

A GARDEN PRIVY

Unsung and un-thought of at bottom of garden
The basic, simple privy is no burden
Now it doubles as a cosy garden store
And a port of call as of yore!
Share your time with many wild creatures
As you ponder and think of it's features -
Peeling paint, ivy clad window, creaky door,
Cut sheets of newspaper and on the floor
A hedgehog hunts for grubs and pests
As blackbird arrives with full beak at it's nest
To feed the young it hopes to rear
And warn off the moggy that's too near!

Time finished on the throne of thrones;
Close door against invading ivy grown
So strong as it makes the privy it's own
Whilst the rhubarb plants, not long sown,
Will provide many a pie and crumble
On the brightly coloured old kitchen table.
Cottage pensioner sits on stool and stares
As collie dog, lifelong friend, - what a pair -
Curls up satisfied on mat by ancient door
As guardian of master and much more!
The crafty black cat still watches at privy
As the blackbird settles on nest so comfy.
The humble brick privy watches over all
As wildlife calls it a day and the sun does fall.

Hail to thee blithe privy!

A LONDON SUBURBAN TRAVELLER.

L eave front door with reluctance
'Have a good day'
'I won't'

Early morning walk with briefcase
Beside London's canalised water system
To a joyous queue of familiar faces
Waiting for the odious set of blue carriages
And uncared diesel engine to
Carry like-minded , numbed and
Routine suburban travellers to their mundane
Daily nine to five jobs in the city.
A station announcer sounding just as
Bored with routine reminds commuters
That they stand at Palmers Green -
As if they needed reminding - for a train
Calling at all stations to Moorgate
That god forsaken hell hole
At the buffers of the line.

Carriage doors slam and guard's
Whistles shriek at this early hour as
Commuters stare across rusting railway tracks
To roofs and gardens of suburban houses,
Church towers and spires, small parks
And suburban roads jammed with cars and
Red London buses all on their
Dreary and dull routine.
Bowes Park flies by as the grim suburban
Train joins it's larger and far more
Important brothers and sisters as we
Pass 'alley palley', dear home
Once of the friendly Beeb.

More crashing of doors and piercing
Whistles as hoards of automatons join
The already bored mass of travellers
Glued to their Times newspaper or
Struggling to fathom the crossword!
Many still stare vacantly out of the
Grime laden windows of the non compartment
Carriages or at luggage racks above a
Row of fellow passengers most likely
Wishing they were on a beach in Spain!

Have we stopped at stupendous Finsbury Park ?
Of course we have – there's no more room!
Past Hornsey and Haringey and
Great Uncle and Aunt's much
Celebrated haunt at Turnpike Lane.
Diesel fumes fill the carriages as
An Edinburgh express rushes by in a
Tunnel with clatter and roar and
The flashing of carriage lights.
Onward through Copenhagen and Gasworks
Tunnels into the smoky atmosphere of a
Filthy, grime laden suburban Kings Cross.

Gulp for air before the merry
Entourage descends into the bowels of
Suburban London – 'The Drain', I believe,
Through a series of filthy tunnels to
Emerge, still on automatic pilot, at
Farringdon's light and airy canopied
Station open at last to sky and clouds
To greet those grimed and weary
Travellers leaving the train.

Amidst clatter of doors and whine of
The arrival of a Metropolitan Underground
Train bound for leafy, suburban Ruislip.
Workers continue their monotonous daily
Routine to the tedium of the office desk.

Past persons of the Hebrew faith slinking in
Dark doorways clothed in black overcoats and
Homburgs, stroking jet black full length beards
No doubt considering their next acquisition and
Sale of precious stones in the shady, secretive
World of Hatton Gardens, the Diamond Quarter.

The drawing board and angle poise lamp
Are still there along with the drawings
Worked on so steadfastly from the day before.
From the window legal wizards and clerks
Are seen strutting from door to door
Across grassed and flowered gardens
Bundles of pink ribboned documents
Tucked under their arm – nothing has changed!

Noonday relief comes with walk to
Browse the dusty shelves of some tiny
And packed antiquarian bookshop in a
Lane close to the frantic traffic of Euston Road.
Clutch ancient leather bound volume back to
The office down Gray's Inn Road.

The afternoon drags on with just a
Cup of tea and Lincoln[s] [Inn] biscuit to
Liven up the boredom before the
Monotonous routine starts all over again.
Past Hatton Gardens - least like a garden.
Past familiar faces outside Farringdon Station;
Acquisition of the London Evening Standard
Almost a signature of the city worker.
The briefcase, carrying remains of sandwiches,
Essential to give that air of authority!

Into the same dingy blue carriages and
With the same bleary eyed engine crew
This time bound for Hertford North
Stopping at all stations in between.
Tired of life, bored and staring

Passengers complete the daily routine
But no Times crossword to struggle with
The Evening Standard offering obviously no match.
Once more alight at home station
Walk with briefcase and paper tucked under arm
The same roads and paths, so numbed
By the tedium and boredom of the day
The change in street name is not noticed!
Key in front door
'Had a good day?'
'I haven't.'
'Remember this weekend we visit mother-in-law.'
Visions of a very fat, trotting hippopotamus.
'What's for tea?'
'Your usual.'

MOROCCO AND THE MARRAKECH EXPRESS

F lying into Agadir a coastal city
　　Of some grandeur one might cast a tear
　　As you pass over what was once the
Epicentre of old city and quake which hit
So hard the people and caused catastrophe.
Like Pompeii, but not with molten ash,
The quake it did destroy it's ancient walls
And fine buildings once so proud on hill
Overlooking the sea – such a great pity!

There remains within this capital
Ancient souks, bazaars and alleyways
Teeming with Moroccan traders and snake
Charmers of all faiths and nationalities
Bartering spices, carpets and even animals.
A mystic haze hangs over the stalls
And secretive alleys where you are invited
To have your fortune told or be entertained
By beautiful belly dancers exposing almost all!

We board a coach to cross Atlas Mountains
Through snow laden peaks bright
With the pink blossom of almond trees
And are amazed at the sight we now see -
Desert with palms and life giving fountains,
Past workers with Christ's donkey and cart
Laden with goods for market and camels
Plodding manfully forward as man and child
Build mud house beneath shadow of mountain.

By the side of the sand strewn street
We pass the Marrakech railway of
Worldwide renown, but there is little
Sign of the Marrakech Express in
The energy sapping Moroccan heat.
What a pleasure to enter the cool of

A hotel arched courtyard with
Lily strewn pond and fountain; and then
We eat Moroccan cus – cus . What a treat!

Sword and flame swallowers entertain
And even more belly dancers parade
Amidst musicians and snake charmers
As we drink the local Maroc red wine
So potent we try to stay sober but in vain.
A little worse for wear after the pleasures
Laid on by our Moroccan hosts
We once more attempt to board the coach
To cross desert for snowy Atlas Mountains!

A spectacular electric storm rolls along
The flat desert plains as we leave town
And head tired and befuddled back to Agadir
Across the snow capped peaks
Clutching prize purchases and possessions among
Our neighbour holiday makers on the coach.
Light has fallen and below lies Agadir all lit up
As the coach drops weary folk at hotel
Where we're reasonably sure we belong!

TUSCANY, OSTERIAS AND SUNFLOWERS

T his is the town of Pisa – what a shock!
Nothing but the Leaning Tower and Duomo
To which many thousand tourists do flock
And gaze and wonder – and then go!

Better travel South into deepest Tuscany
Avoiding mad drivers who seem hell bent
On forcing you to leave and seek some tea
To relieve the stress that's not heaven
sent!

The villa and pool lie by side of hill
Which sunflowers and sheep with bells do fill.
A pool where 'lobsters' plunge and parade
And 'fry' on nearby sunbeds – what a charade!

Ancient cities of Florence and Sienna -
A sight to see amidst all their chaos!
Don't forget the meal at the villa osteria -
We must ensure we don't get lost!

Stand and admire the Ponte Vecchio bridge
Steeped in history and famed goldsmith's shops
And then the medieval pageantry of Sienna's image
When bare back riders career and do not stop!

Sienna's 'palio' in city square is some sight to see,
But we must move on as we're late for tea!
It's not too late to visit a hilltop town or two -
Perhaps Volterra, Colle Alta or San Gimigiano.

We leave the hilltop fortified towns today
And retire gracefully to the villa and food
To spend time gazing across and away
Over olive grove and vineyard clad hills - we feel so good!

As 'early birds' we make our way in a hurry
To Volterra, volcanic and gastronomic delight,
And then to San Gimigiano, the 'Delle Belle Torri'
With medieval tower skyline so perfect and right.

We sip Vino Nobile and consume an Italian 'dish'
To look out across courtyard, water and wish
That we could be here for ever more
As the sun sets in golden ball of fire.

Hilltop villages at heart of Chianti Classico
Are quaint and small with chapel and call bell
At their little centre where sheep may go
But little else moves as far as we can tell!

A glorious day is spent on the Tuscany coast
In crystal clear seas adventure skin diving
Suit, mask and flippers donned we don't toast
In baking sun but find sea life so amazing!

Our last night is spent at osteria by candlelight
Where serving wench ensures we dine well upon
All manner of Tuscan food and wine into the night
Only to be told our waitress comes from Swindon!

We don't want to leave as we consume more wine
But know our time has come to finish our dine,
Walk contentedly back to villa as crickets
Call under starlit balmy Tuscan night sky.
We need our sleep but there's no peace for the wicked!

EBORACUM, MICKLEGATE AND No.19

Grab tickets and briefcase – what a chore!
Exit mews by bright red front door.
Board the 'tube' at Oxford Circus on the
Central Line amongst weary commuters.
Hop off so soon at Tottenham Court Road
To join the trains of the Piccadilly Line.
Crushed and squashed in – what a fuss,
But soon we all fall out as it is King's Cross.

Already exhausted and tired of the throngs
I'm swept forward to station concourse along
Winding passages, steps and escalators
Until, at a gate, my ticket is clipped.
I gather my thoughts as Cubitt's train arches
Come into view and head straightway
For Platform 4 where train with Pullman cars
Awaits to leave for Eboracum, not that far!

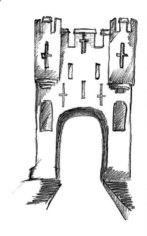

Micklegate Bar, Yo...

Once in plush seats I look forward to breakfast
And relax and enjoy as time goes so fast.
We're leaving King's Cross through dingy tunnels
But soon pass through bright countryside aplenty!
Breakfast is served – what a repast!
The tea is divine poured from silver teapot.
Stations and fields fly by as we gather speed
And head for first stop – Doncaster, indeed!

Past sidings and old buildings we move on North
Alongside power stations and slag heaps, little worth
It seems as I feel so full from breakfast consumed.
I collect all baggage as the train slows down
For entry to Eboracum – a city so fair
With Minster and Shambles – such a glorious place!
Under York's vast train shed I hand
My ticket to the collector – and just stand!

What a view with magnificent Minster behind;
City walls and banks of daffodils so kind
To the eye after travelling at speed
From the 'Big Smoke' to such a city
So full of history and proud buildings -
A delight to ponder and walk through.
I make my way down under Micklegate Bar
And note antiquarian bookshops – not that far!

Meetings done and with lunchbox in hand
I head off to bookshops – antiquarian and secondhand.
With leather bound purchases in brown paper bag
I walk by gentle Ouse and then
Round Clifford's Tower as briskly I stride
Back to Micklegate for another 'meet.'
With time to spare before my train calls
I set off towards Minster before eve doth fall.

Down ancient Swinegate I become side tracked
As a little lane draws me back.
With cobbled way and jettied buildings
Grape Lane still holds it's mysterious feel
Even though notorious brothels have long since
Gone leaving tiny timber framed building,
No.19 tucked in one corner producing
Fine cuisine in idyllic setting.

The time has come to leave and look
For afternoon train with my books and
First Class travel, so comforting.
With own compartment and silver
Service to compliment smooth journey
Afternoon tea is served with fruit
Cake cut to order by kindly train folk
As we return once more to the grim 'Big Smoke'.

RATAE CORITANORUM AND GREYFRIARS RICHARD

ome to the 'Foxes' and Filbert Street ground
The city team adorned in blue abound
Whilst locals eat sarnies in Town Hall Square
And the nearby market sell apple and pear,
Grapefruit, oranges, grapes and more
Sold off to students as such cheap fare
At end of day as workers wend way home
And office staff hang up the infernal phone.
The city falls asleep as eve draws near
And birds go to roost with no fear.
Lights now twinkle across the city
As vagrants search for shelter - what a pity.
The car park has emptied at nearby Greyfriars.
There is little to shout about even for town criers.

The remains of a King can now rest in peace -
Laid beneath concrete all in one piece
Until one day they search for his soul
With pick axe and shovel while many call foul.
The King is found, the cry goes out -
All his remains or thereabouts.
Richard III fell at Bosworth Field -
Hurriedly buried away from well heeled.
Lost and forgotten beside the Greyfriars
Then sadly covered by acres of cars!
Few thought that when he was found
Words between Eboracum and Coritanorum would abound
As to where his remains should finally be laid.
Homage to Richard from the Dioceses was paid
Each fighting with rhetoric until York gave in
To lose the 'Battle of the Roses' - no win!
Richard will be buried at Cathedral in Leicester
Yet still the arguments continue to fester.
Being at rest and peace is the main aim,
Not forgotten for his historic fame.

THE WHITE LADY

T he White Lady ghost
Has been seen many a time
Walking the wards
Giving compassion and care
To those who need it most
Probably even at Soho Square
An outlier of The Middlesex Hospital scene.
Though many buildings have been on the site
She still appears in spite
Of different floor levels -
Lower half one ward, head and shoulders another!
It does not seem to cause any bother.
Her ghost glides and smoothly travels
From ward to ward with sorrowful eye
Helping those in pain to gracefully die
On wings of prayer up to the sky.

*The Middlesex Hospital
Coat of Arms*

AN OLD STEAM ENGINE

My fire is spent
My life has ebbed away
I once spewed fire and smoke
As I climbed peak and hill
Past lambs frolicking in the fields
My days are done
As a giant of the iron road
Boiler, buffers and tender
Crudely cut up for scrap
And now I am found
In some washing machine or car
Rest in pieces!

FRANCIS AND THE 'WESTERN' SUNSET

The blood red sun sets in the sky
Reflecting on tracks and trains that try
To move their heavy loads toward
The bridge as keen spotters lean forward
To try to gain the number and name –
'Defiant' or 'Western Glory' – what a game!
In the half light of fast fading day
Many have gone past their allotted stay.
It must be a 'Western' – hear it roar -
Two Maybach engines full throttle to the fore
And clouds of exhaust pour into sky
Now crystal clear as it must try
To haul it's passengers to Paddington Station.
There can be no excuse nor hesitation!
Another 'Western' nearby 'shouts to the sky'
As it leaves station with loaded stone by
Tortuous bank to tiny Dilton Marsh Halt
Working flat out with every effort - not at fault!

The night draws in; the tracks at peace.
It's time to meet Francis who's on his feet
At the depot lit brightly by piercing white lamps
Where diesels lie idle and Francis stamps
His feet against the biting winter cold
But suggests we go inside and be bold
To have a cuppa made by Steve his mate
To accompany mince pies set neatly on plate!
Fortified against the oncoming bitter cold
We are given the precious 'keys' to hold -
'Keys' that can make beast out of diesel,
As he rummages through his coat - what upheaval!
With great coat, anoraks and gloves tucked in
We climb down from office close to oil bin
Set beside a row of simmering locos.
All wait to be checked as enthusiast photos
Them with elaborate gear for his collection
And we find more locos closer to the station

All ready to be started up for next journey
Into dark cold night to Witham Friary,
Merehead, Botley, Northampton and Acton
With many stone wagons - a full load on.
Francis climbs aboard a 'Western'diesel
Which starts with a roar and black smoke so evil!
'Druid', 'Stalwart', 'Patriarch' and there's 'Dragoon'
All coming to life's end and breaker's yard so soon.
Inside the cab of 'Emperor' we glide
Down depot tracks with Francis at our side
To place the 'Western' in first position
Ready to take early commuters from the station
To day's work in 'Big Smoke' at Paddington
And return to depot with stone from yard at Acton.
'Lord' and 'Lady' are lined up next for the fray
Ahead of hauling loaded stone – no delay,
As 'Duke' and 'Venturer' come in for a rest
Since Francis' mates know what's best
For tired engines that have done their
stint.
Depot workers now call it a day for well
earned pint!

The sun does rise in the eastern sky.
It's another day for the 'Westerns'
who will try
Their hardest until the end of the road
Hauling passengers and stone by the
load.
Most will finish their days as scrap
Even though they have soul and heart –
so cheap
To railway bosses – just a heap of steel!
They're not fussed – they have no feel1
Just a matter of pounds, shillings and pence
For twisted heap of metal beyond the fence.
Sadly, great cousin Francis, the ferryman is no more.
Gone to meet his engine in the sky – for
All I know it could be 'Western Lady'
Even a Hall, Castle, saddle tank or Prairie.
His beloved 'Westerns' have met their fate

As rusting hulks at Swindon is their state
Like Francis they'll never be forgotten
Hearts of gold they had – we were smitten
By their personality and favour
'Western Delight' we will always savour
From Paddington to Exeter and Penzance we met.
For Francis and 'The Western' it is their sunset.

CHARLIE AND THE SIGNAL BOX

I t be a bright, fine and sunny day
As we make our way past yesterday's hay
Lying in giant rolls across Somerset
Fields towards a signal box that has yet
To reach it's peak of traffic and activity
When passenger and freight vie to see
Who can reach the junction first.
Charlie's signals are at danger, his thirst
Can only be quenched by a cup of tea.
As we climb signal box steps and see
He's already feet up in the easy chair.
There are no trains 'in section', to be fair!
Branch line tablet machine sits merrily
In the corner with loo roll on it for company!

Charlie suddenly lifts from chair as bell
Clatters, then levers slam – who can tell
What it all means – we're not sure.
But Charlie sees one train through and more
Booked to pass his box at Witham Friary.
Both express and stone we shall see.
We sit down with cuppa before the fray
As Charlie answers bells he doth pray
The fast passenger will pass before stone
Trains by the dozen arrive – he phones
Quarry and Blatchbridge Junctions to plea
They hold them back while he sups his tea!
His prayers are answered by mate at Clink
Who tells him a stone train is 'on the blink'.
Thank God for that as he takes the tablet
To Branch line stone as others queue to get
On to load their own – then rings the phone –
It's the 'gnome' at Quarry who loves 'dog and bone'
'But not when it's so busy' Charlie chimes.
As levers clatter and bells do ring so sublime
The Friary box is worked to the very limit
As we work hard to make toast and buttered crumpet

For Charlie to eat when he has a minute to spare
Or for us with tea - it's signal box fare.
Levers slam while signals go up and down
As 'Hoover' roars past heading for 'town'
And a much loved 'Western' waits in loop at Friary
With stone bound for Brentford, Acton or Botley.
An empty stone waits with 'Western Dragoon'
To climb Branch line to Quarry all so soon;
Charlie hands Branch line tablet to the train
And chats to driver and mate who both complain
Of the many trains and too little time
To persuade diesels to valiantly make incline.
'Western' diesels are Charlie's favourite -
'Ranger', 'Hussar', 'Firebrand' and 'Gauntlet,'
'Cavalier', 'Sultan', 'Musketeer' and 'Viceroy' -
All have travelled this way to Witham Friary.

Charlie's shift is at an end, his day is over
And we make our way back to cars, by clover
Field bright with colour and red poppy
By the church once a Medieval Monastery
As a double headed ballast train does meet
A 'Western' shouting to the sky so sweet
Hauling stone wagons up steep Branch incline.
There'll be plenty of smoke but she'll be fine!
Charlie's mate will care for trains and box
On a cold but busy night with thick woolly socks
To keep out the frost as well as cuppa tea
Ensures bells and levers remain a total mystery!

Sadly the signal box at Friary is no more
Replaced with lifeless colour lights to the fore.
But memories of Charlie and the box linger long -
'Never to be forgotten' shall be our Somerset song!

FRED AND HAIRY NED

I stand as eager child at village shop
Straining to look in window before I drop
With crash to path only to rise again
On stone steps in spite of the rain!
Set on display amongst packets and plates
Are tins and boxes of delightful chocolates
With not to be missed pictures of cottages of late
while sentinel cat and dog stand at garden gate.
Drool over chocolate box with cottage under thatch -
Other houses on tin and box are not a patch
But even such country scenes should not bother
Us yet there's trouble at them thar' thatcher!

Enter stage right the cottage of Finkle Lane
Sold to couple under no illusion of the strain
It would prove on pocket, body and soul
Not least extracting Russian Vine so foul;
Old timber shed and sprawling dead tree -
Hope someone would collect both for free!
A diminutive timber frame cottage at that
Still sporting remains of local thatched 'hat'.

What a delight to cast the eye upon - no sham,
But a special example of the local craftsman
Who put heart and soul into it some 400 years back
Like the old gentleman, scarf tight at neck
And brightly coloured woolly gloves on hands,
Arthritis wracked by years of hard work who stands
Watching thatcher lift bundles with fork
To fellow craftsmen on roof weaving their magic
With liggers, sways, spurs and stays – a habit
The old gentleman had been used to for years
At his own thatching firm. Now in tears
Fred recalled as he stood in the lane
His time on Finkle Lane cottage and the fame
That went with his work on the eaves 'roll'
Now just a lump of wood called arris rail!

One day Fred Oldfield no longer stood there.
Like his thatching firm Fred was no more
And the unique thatching' dialect' of his stock
Working on old roofs akin to darning a large sock
As Celtic thatch held by a network of ropes
To secure roof against storms you hoped!
Sadly the' knitting' often came apart
To find the roof blown away and then to start
Bundling reeds onto the roof before bed -
Remember to tie it all down with 'hairy ned'.

A thatched cottage keeps you warm, for sure
But certainly in pocket quite poor!
To live in Honeyway Cottage off Finkle Lane
Was a pleasure to be part of history and fame!

AN OLD WELSH LONGHOUSE

U nder the brow of a large hill
The old Welsh longhouse stands still -
Gaunt, thick sandstone walls
And room after room cascades like falls
As a young stream down mountain side.
The house is aged but full of pride

As Quakers once married and baptised
Inside it's walls and many tried
To make a living off the land
With only farmer and a young farmhand
Milking the cows and tending the sheep
For hour on end before they fell asleep.
Tupping, shearing, lambing, the lot
Farmer then hired shepherd on the spot
To keep the flock spick and span
And drive to market whenever he can.
Farmer's wife and daughter kept house
More than likely in company of many a mouse!

Troedyrhiw Fawr

We've been resident for some twenty years
And with our sheep suffered plenty of tears.
A loss at lambing is so hard to take -
To dig the hole for the sheep - it's fate.
Great joy when ewe delivers twins;
We're over the moon on shepherd's wings!
We've been through such a lot whilst there
But the old, homely house holds no fear
For us in joy and sorrow in the bower
Of the friendly and peaceful Troedyrhiw Fawr.

We must move on as bodies grow old
And wish the old house good luck and be bold
For new owners who now come behind.
May they in peace tread the boards and find
Good fortune, happiness and health
Remember – your time is short upon this earth!

AN ORPHANED LAMB

Just a small bundle of wrinkled wool
Lying, bleating in the foot well
Of a battered old farm van.
Gathered up in comfy woollen blankets
And placed in a box in the
Warming oven of the old Aga.

Drunk the bottle dry and fallen to sleep
We leave the little one for the night
To be woken early on
By bleating and clatter of tiny feet
On the tiled kitchen floor
Surprised she had survived.

Through thick and thin she soldiered on
To reach the ripe old age of seventeen!
Laid to rest in the Middle Meadow
Amidst all her friends
Sometime earlier
Meeting in woolly heaven.

THE HEAVENLY SCILLY ISLES

From the air a stunning and beautiful archipelago
Set as a tropical paradise in a world of it's own.
Endless sparkling white beaches and azure blue
Waters, blissful peace and pure serenity, few
Would question such a rarity in the whole world
Nestling in the middle of 'nowhere'- watch it unfold!

Pick up bike or even a horse for your picnic feast.
Few cars, no noise or thumping music – just peace.
Take care of your food, even if only an apple
As Scillonian horses, our friends, love to snaffle!
Cross crystal clear waters by island boat
Followed by seals and seabirds far worse than a goat!
Sampson and Bryher's waters are brilliantly clear
Perfect for snorkelling or lazy swim – no fear.
Hitch up at St Agnes below the Turks Head -
Time for cold beer, scrumpy and being fed

Whilst young girl walks through glass blue
Shallows seeking the shells of wondrous hue.
Relax, unwind by crystalline white sand
In unspoilt cove with luscious scones and
Strawberry jam with thick yellow cream now
Served courtesy of the local Jersey cow!

St. Martins - so friendly, peaceful and timeless;
Crystal clear light and parchment sands endless
With no one there you're tempted to swim or snorkel
If you can take your eyes off 'Neck of the Pool'
And 'Lawrence's Brow' spectacular coastal scenery
Before being tempted by cream tea at cottage café.
Walk over island's cricket square at Higher Town Bay
And join John Graham at his vineyard and stay
Long enough to savour superb, cooled wine
And soak up baking sun so good for the vine.
Ample wine to take past no Customs and Excise -
It's time to leave for St. Mary's to be precise.
Back on St.Mary's tis time to explore miles
Of scenic coastal paths that will make you smile
At the sub tropical flowers that do abound
Whether by pathway, cliff or granite mound.
From Porthcressa and Pendinnis to Old Town Bay
Down by Gull Rock the views make you wish to stay
Forever by this Paradise on Earth which even
Harold Wilson wisely felt was his heaven
Such that the little church by the sea
Is his chosen resting place to finally be.

Another day, another walk by Buzza Tower
Highest point for many a mile and a shower
Does not spoil splendid views to Samson and Tresco
Across silvery seas to St. Agnes and Gugh. But
Behold, a tiny cottage with red phone box in gardens,
Natural and un- manicured with sign 'Scilly Sea Urchins'.
By the wicket gate a fine piece of nostalgia -
Black and white name board simply saying 'Nowhere'.
To the front an unbecoming timber shed
With sign - 'Island Sea Safaris' affixed -
Snorkelling with seals, gig race trips and sea safaris -

Enchanting adventures led by Mark and Susie.
Mask, flippers and wetsuit donned so quickly
We embark on adventure to the 'garden of the sea'.
Be it sea garden or cottage garden so free
You must return to see them and the seals like me.
The Scillies 'heaven' enchanting and so fair
It is truly heaven and heaven is 'nowhere'.

THE QUANTOCKS AND KILVE SHORE

'No lovelier hills have eased my weary thoughts to rest
All so wild and beautiful as ever have been painted'.

To Kilve shore we must now head
But not before stomachs are well fed!
Down wildflower strewn winding lane
Gently dipping to Kilve shore line.
But oh look – there's a sign - 'Cream Teas'
Just past the embattled church amidst trees.
The building looks rather in need
So decide to support and have a feed.
Through rose laden bower to delightful garden
With fancy tables and chairs – this is no burden
As we enter enchanting Kilve Chantry
Where scrumptious food is kept in their pantry.
Earl Grey Tea, strawberry jam scones and
Cream - a delight! But are we able to stand,
Lift ourselves from glorious food
And garden to be in the mood
To fight the flab and walk to the shore
And look out to sea as Wordsworth saw
Many a rigged vessel plying it's trade
Before the evening drew in and sky did fade.
The shore is smooth, the sea is green
And many a creature in rock pools to be seen.

A lazy walk up winding lane from the sea
Past the Chantry now closing for tea,
Through bright array of wildflowers by farms
To drag tired body into the Hood Arms.
Collapse in heap - we've been so far
And must have a welcome pint at the bar!

THE 'THANKFUL VILLAGE' OF AISHOLT

Aisholt in Quantocks is charm and delight
Like St.Just in Roseland might
Compare in deepest Cornish estuary.
But Aisholt is 'blessed' and most happy
As eight of it's young men went to war
And all came back home to lean on bar,
At the local inn amidst the hills
Trying to forget their horrendous ills.

Thus be ye thankful to the good Lord
For those men called to first War of World
Have returned to their devoted families
After years in the crippling trenches.
Many are not complete in body and mind
But Aisholt thanks the veterans and find
Ways to remember them as heroes
With stone memorial to their souls
Who rest in peace overlooking Will's Neck
They remembered from childhood days, by heck!
Aisholt like Arkholme hear no 'last post'
As they are thankful for being spared the loss.

THE TOLLERS

Toller Fratrum Church

e it Whelme or be it Fratrum
They're so much like nearby
Rampisham.
Down narrow lane on beaten track
Once going down there's no turn-
ing back!

Toller Whelme is not plain to see
Hidden in steep valley in deep mystery.
Just the old house, a cottage and church
Through ivy clad gate and not much
Else but few gravestones for locals at rest
And a blackbird perched thoughtfully on her nest
In the old porch for those to enter in.
Alas no key unless you're very thin
To squeeze thro' door eaten away
By moth and worm – probably another day!

Fratrum sits upon rural chalk down
With views across to Dorchester town.
So isolated, lost, but peaceful and small
Once found, hamlet and church will enthral.
Single cell church so sweet and so dear,
St. Basil alongside old manor and barn, a mere
Thatched cottage and post box nearby -
A postman, once a week, must fly by
Down narrow lane above Hooke river
As it ends in a field he can go no further!
Only monks and brothers found this a haven
As St. Basils' is mobbed by rook and raven.
Little moves in Fratrum today
But it's worth a visit any day
To pay respect to Brother Knights of St John
Whose old thatched barn is so woebegone.

One thing you cannot better follow
Are the lanes to Fratrum Toller and'Whelme in the Hollow'.

WRAXALL AND POET JOHN MILTON

Tis a goodly, bright Spring morning
   The lark is singing high.
   The dew is long since gone.
Another fine country day is dawning.

The sheep are in the meadow.
Cattle drink by the edge of the pond
As butterflies and bees hover nearby.
Day creeps up on Wraxall so slow!

It is such a sleepy hamlet
Of barns, Manor House and cott
One could almost say John Milton
Was still here as a rural poet.

Blind Milton came to Wraxall as a friend
Soaking up pleasures at the Manor.
He'd spend his time a'walking far
Always sorry to leave Wraxall behind.

To Rampisham and Uphall were his usual way
But often went on to Charity Bottom,
Even Evershot and Frome St. Quintin.
There were no limits during his stay.

His time with William Lawrence was so precious;
He loved the Dorset Countryside
Where with Will. he wandered as a summer cloud
Before his time had come and he be called to rest.

CATTISTOCK, GGS*, ST. PETER AND ST.PAUL

P ast Maiden Newton and The Bakery** yum, yum;
Alongside the railway and the babbling Frome;
By Combe Bottom and Wessex Ridgeway far
From Dorchester and road traffic's incessant hum.

When I visit, the village sleeps soundly.
Even The Fox and Hounds - centre of the community,
Snoozes peacefully in warm summer sun
Whilst Church to St.Peter and Paul stands so stately,

Proudly overlooking winding village streets.
It is so masterful and a perfect GGS* design
In so small and beautifully intimate village;
St.Peter and St. Paul's place is so natural a feat.

It is a wondrous delight to walk down
Winding lanes of pleasing vernacular cotts
And admire St. Peter and St. Paul's from afar
With glorious backdrop of Ridgeway and chalk downs.

I end my walk in the churchyard green and
Pleasingly solemn beneath the wonderful
Tower and baptistery of GGS's * inspiration
As rooks and crows gather as a band.

I meet the church organist on her way
To practice on the 'ivories' in the loft.
She tells me how the village must fund
Works or they will have nowhere to pray.

I leave Cattistock slumbering in peace
I'll be back for a pint at The Fox and Hounds
And I'm sure the Church will still be there
Lying below Castle and Norden Hills – what a place!

*GGS – George Gilbert Scott Jnr., Architect
**The Bakery, Maiden Newton is sadly now closed

Cattistock church

ST. NICHOLAS'* SANCTITY AND SOLEMNITY

Through a gap in bedecked hedgerow
Deep in the grassy Blackmore Vale
Close to the Friary and sheltered by Gore Hill
A dear little church lost in waving grass meadow.

I sat me down amidst banks of wild flowers
On the warm summer grass of churchyard
So small in deepest rural Dorset.
Peaceful and at rest in this delightful bower.
Bees and butterflies hover across God's Acre
As those 'called' lie in solitude and rest
With simple stone to mark their repose
Beside St. Nicholas at Hilfield and their maker.

Inside the sanctuary it's peace and quietness
Where every pew has magnificent carving
From dragons to the Evangelists and Christ
On a donkey – it makes one feel so pious.

I do not want to leave the solitude of Hilfield
But rest awhile to contemplate and pray
That when my time should come
It is peaceful and beautiful as this green field.

*St. Nicholas, Hilfield, Dorset

THE CAPITAL OF MARSHWOOD VALE

Beside the River Char and overlooking
The glorious Vale of Marshwood
In West Dorset lies an ancient village
Rather sprawling but nonetheless enchanting.

Oft called 'Capital of Marshwood Vale'
Whitchurch Canonicorum is no proper match
For the stupendous and true magnificence
Of it's church that hides a mysterious tale.

The church dedicated to St. Candida or Wite
Displays a unique mandorla stone shrine
That holds the bones of it's patron saint
Killed in massacre at Dockum in a fight.

Hierarchy at the church made so sure
That copious sums of votif money were taken
From pilgrims visiting shrine to pray,
Heal strange diseases and seek a cure.

'Tis little wonder that the gilded chest
Of monies and jewels ensured church grew
Whilst parishioner George Summers inspired
Mr Shakespeare to pen his masterpiece 'The Tempest'!

All is quite as the Char makes to the sea
At Charmouth whilst dear little thatched
Cottages 'midst country lanes nestle
As good neighbours and friendly company.

On crossroads of the lane leading out
To Baker's Cross and Berne Farm
A group of ancient houses
Huddle together as soul mate cotts.

Old Cross Cottage and neighbour nearby
On Berne Lane both sport dear thatched

Porches with wicker seat for incumbent
Amidst country gardens tended so neatly.

Whitchurch Canonicorum is blessed amongst many;
Not even Morcombelake or Ryall close by can vie
With the perfect peace and splendid church
Nor can Chideock or Wootton Fitzpaine nearby.

Most favoured of villages cannot fail
To impress visitors as they stroll the lanes.
Long may you remain at heart of St. Candida and Cross,
Undoubted Capital of fine Marshwood Vale.

St. Wite's mandorla

THE DORSET ASKER

he Asker swiftly flows in
Meadows green and so serene
Past Bradpole, Loders and Spyway Inn;
Through deep valley at Askerswell it's been
Starting life deep in the Downs
At Stancombe Farm - it knows no bounds.

In old age it joins the Brit
At Skilling Hill by the brewery.
Home of fine cask ales fit
For a king or those who passeth by.
From the thatched brewhouse
Asker and Brit conjoined, meander
Past Bothenhampton as quiet as a mouse
To reach the sea and anchor
At West Bay, once fishing port you see
Where dear little cots still look out to sea.

Footbridge at Askerswell

DEAR ASKERSWELL

Down steep and hedge lined lane
You come upon dear Askerswell
Deep in a glorious verdant dell
With St.Michael's tower and weather vane.

Sheltered amidst a canopy of trees
Since medieval times the tower
And church bedecked with wild flowers
As some pay homage upon their knees.

No shop, no pub is in the 'well'
Just fast flowing Asker passes thru'
From high in hills it doth brew
Whilst Spyway pub looks down into dell.

The Spyway Inn - a splendid place
Where tales of field and fireside are commonly told
And stupendous cask ales you can behold
All set below Eggerdon —what a place!

Older than Domesday by many a mile
Parson Barnes would spin a poem
Of common folk who made it home
Whilst Thomas Hardy made them smile.

Past mill and cottage by the Asker
It's best not to linger for too long
As heavy snowfall may prove you
wrong.
Stuck in the Spyway for
oh so long!

Askerswell Church

THE BELLS OF ST.MARY'S

T he bells of St.Mary's ring out so clear
　　Calling the faithful to humble prayer.
　　An aged priest stands by the door
To welcome participants, so few yet not
so poor.

Priest 'speeds' off to local inn for well earned pint
To prepare for afternoon christening at the font
With parents, folks and generous baby carriage.
Then to evensong with organist, if he can manage
The whinging bellows and clattering ivory keys
As ancient choristers do puff and wheeze!

St.Mary's is a rich and bounteous benefice
But few participate in daily services thrice
Apart from the occasional and religious church mice.
With matins and evensong collection oh so meagre
As wicked gargoyles look down in anger
And verger counts just enough to buy a burger!

Good ladies prepare church for coming Eastertide
Garnishing everywhere with dignity and pride -
The altar adorned with cloth and arum lily.
Be prepared – Easter is forecast to be so chilly!

Easter comes and Easter goes
And cherry blossom falls to the ground
As St.Mary's gets in the throws
For next festival – one of many that do abound.

The bells of St. Mary's ring out so clear
Come all ye faithful people, come ye to prayer.

ANCIENT BRIDPORT AND BURGAGES

Tucked behind delightful Medieval charm
Of ancient Bridport market town
Lie lanes and burgages that have grown
In centuries to become home to rope walkers.
A cottage industry that became the norm
To help all those ships weather the storm!

Down Folly Mill Lane, ancient thoroughfare
So narrow and winding – just room for a cart –
To meet Asker water meadows where they do start;
Where once stood Folly Mil so true and fare
That milled the flax in buildings ravaged by worm
To help all those ships weather the storm!

Little is left but dear stone cottage
That now fronts onto Back Rivers Lane.
The mill leet is no more – not in the frame –
Leet bridge vanquished; no cottagers do forage.
The lane goes straight on over filled in leet
To meet the River Asker by pleasant seat!

The gardens on leet long since filled in
Are wondrous to behold with every spring -
Cherry and May blossom, the scent a
glorious thing.
And burgage plots are self sufficiency garden
As burgagees dig and add some peat.
To meet the River Asker by
pleasant seat!

SPRINGTIME IN DEEP DORSET COUNTRYSIDE

T all grasses waving gently in the light Spring breeze
As blackbird and warbler search the meadow flowers
For food for fledglings on the nest.
Butterflies and bees drift
From flower to flower
Around the sacred and hallowed ground
Where many locals have been laid to rest
Amidst God's Acre in peace.

Gravestones shimmer through the midday heat
Amongst delicate Lady's Smock and sticky Bedstraw
Vetch and clover
As the old church bell tolls the hour
And Dorset countryside sleeps under warm and pleasing sun.
A gentleman with stick sits by the village green

And ponders on life's springtime dream
Watching the few who enter the Post Office and shop,
Chew the cud as so many have done.
As mongrel ducks frolic in weed strewn pond
And fast flowing chalk downland stream
The village sleeps once more
Beneath the verdant chalk downs.
Nothing happens. Nothing moves.
Even the gentleman by the green has fallen asleep!

THE STILTON CHEESE AND DORSET KNOB

The morning sun doth rise over village street
In which many hundred onlookers will meet
To witness the mad event that takes place
Outside ancient inn where contestants face
Huge chesses, of Stilton, of course,
That must be rolled to see who's first
To cross the line to win the prize.
 Stilton cheese roller in disguise
Who's wearing a penguin suit, no doubt,
 Accepts the adulations and shouts
To retire to the bar of the ancient inn
For pint of cask ale that's been
So well deserved at the sign
Of the Stilton Cheese that stands so fine
Along the route of Ermine Street ,
Amidst the Cambridgeshire fields full of beet.

Just one minute - we must not delay
But head to Hardy Country and join the fray!

'Tis the first Sunday of the month of May,
A glorious, peaceful sunny Dorset day
When many folk from far and wide
Gather in Cattistock village this Maytide
Beneath the heavenly church tower they meet
To push and jostle the crowd for a seat
So they can witness at first hand
The Dorset Knob Festival and it's band
Playing country tunes as they go
Around the arena of the big knob throw.
Eating, walking, throwing – what fun,
With a hard, crispy knob like a savoury bun!
Some try to pin knob on Cerne Abbas Giant at table

Whilst others throw as darts as far as able!
The sun 'tis setting in the western sky;
The happy knob throwers wave goodbye
For another year ....
They'll be back there is no fear.
Stilton Cheese and Dorset Knob fans so dear!

CROSSBONES AND WINCHESTER GEESE

D own an eerie alley off Redcross Way
Close to bustle of Borough Market – do not stay
Too long as behind rusty old steel gates
Lie 15000 bodies in derelict land, un consecrated.
Beneath inhuman concrete is Crossbones Graveyard
Resting place of outcasts and prostitutes - its hard
To imagine it's chequered history goes back 700 years
And was to be the 'end' and' fears'
Of brothel prostitutes and unwanted children
Who had no Christian burial rites as other brethren.
Few from 'rookeries' and prisons were saved by bell
As they knew they would be thrown into 'hell'.
Prostitutes by Crossbones known as Winchester Geese
Stood little chance but at least
Drunks and thieves from The Globe nearby
And debtors and murderers could try
To escape this awful and foulsome end
Unless in 'clink' they 'went round the bend'.
Close to Tommy's and Guy's of medical stature
All outcasts were good 'meat' for the body snatcher!

Gates to the
Unconsecrated graveyard

A saviour for all those unwanted 'lost souls'
Came to light as a mystic possessed by foul
Or fair means through a 'lost goose' in Crossbones.
John Constable, mystic and playwright, has thrown
All effort in writing and honouring these dead -
The lost and forgotten outcasts ahead
Of building that would destroy for good
The grim but final resting place that stood
To honour very sad souls but human
Beings as ourselves – so go place ribbon
Flowers and votives on the rusty gates
And join the monthly vigil to commemorate
John Constable's 'possession' by a 'lost goose' -
A moving, sad, evocative and atmospheric experience
Just in the shadow of the Shard, masterpiece of science.

APPROACHING AUTUMN

Early morning mists have cleared away
As hazy sun keeps it at bay.
Young children shout and run down lane
Glad to be back at school for Autumn term
While older folks peer out of window pane
At forthcoming autumnal charm
Of fallen beech nuts and golden leaves that do shimmer
Ahead of what could be an Indian summer.
As leaves do shrivel
Once they have burnished
Pull together a pile of rubbish
Just about as it starts to drizzle!
Spirals of smoke from bonfires do arise
As damp leaves and garden waste have no reprise.
Berries are ripe and full of great promise
Blackbird and thrush will face no crisis.
Winds and storms will come before
You can say 'Jack Frost' is at the door.
Enjoy the late summer while you can
Sunny weather is so welcome.
Not long before Autumn turns to Winter -
Freezing hands and solid water!
Frost, snow, hail and ice
We shall all now pay the price.
Little robin – a handsome fellow,
Helps gardeners clear their plots for the winter.
Watch out !You'll get a splinter
From runner bean stakes that I'm sure
And will there be plenty of stinky manure
To feed plants once Spring is here again
When sun will stream through window pane
As trees do grow and birds fly upon the wing.
Hoorah! Once more Spring is arriving!

A RURAL CHURCH AND GOD'S ACRE *

Sacred is the ground upon
Which the old church stands
And has given succour to young and old.
Peace, solitude, isolation and
Tranquillity in deepest Dorset country.
Winding, high hedged lanes and bridleways.
Truly hidden rural gems
Almost lost and forgotten beyond
The overgrown churchyard gate.

Nearby cornfields ripe with harvest
Throb with threshing machines
And the plod of gentle and friendly
Heavy horses gaily decked
With gleaming brasses and bridles.
As villagers bow to the work
Before the Sabbath Day beckons
'Come to Church, all ye good people'
From the distant calling bell.

Families walk the verdant footpath
Bedecked with hosts of wildflowers
As children pick juiciest blackberries
From laden overhanging branches.
Until through the kissing gate
They cross, hand in hand, God's Acre
Where family and friend lie at peace.
To be blessed in the cool sanctuary
By the priest before they return to harvest.

Young children frolic with the stooks
Playing hide and seek and
Chase rabbits into hedgerows
Ablaze with fiery red berries
Before the coming hard winter.

For all seasons the old church
Stands guard over God's Acre.
At peace in snow, sun and rain.
Foxes, badgers butterflies and dragonflies
Move about amidst swaying
Shoulder high grasses in the
Languid, warm breeze
As they have done for centuries past.
Peace reigns in sacred solitude.

**Based on the Church and churchyard at Melbury Bubb, the
little village and nearby fields in Dorset.*

A POOR CHURCH MOUSE

We are poor church mice as you see
Trying to scrape a living for free
Among old hymn books and hassocks we scurry.
To humans we seem to be in such a hurry
Around the organ pipes and keys we go
There's no danger we'll make music below
Our paws are so small and light of touch
But leather of bellows would make a good lunch.
Across the altar and past the candles -
A little wax will do no harm as we dangle
From Easter lilies set in a silver vase.
We are showered by pollen at the base
Of the cross all over the altar cloth
For church cleaners, apart from the moth,
To sort out on their weekly tour of duty
Unless of course they make it all a mystery!

One fine day it irks us to find
Other mice with total pagan mind
Come to Church to take food and wine
But do not partake in Communion – that's fine
As long as they have no proper business here
Us poor church mice will not shed a tear.
Rich field mice invade the choir
But do not worship or have any desire
To share in God's service but just come
To steal hard won fare from our home
And see what we really might be at
In seeing off the inquisitive churchyard cat!
Other mice from fields far, far away
Only come to hear the church organ play
And steal the goods of harvest festival
The only time for church mice to feel full.

The bells do ring - it is so clear
As alarm from mouse home – there is a fear
One of the family has made journey to porch

Where Churchwarden on ladder holding torch
Inspects the roof for signs of an owl.
He need not look far as mice do scowl
At owl pellets across porch floor
That tell you how many mice he's had before!
Best not for mouse to venture further
Or he will surely be owl's next fodder!

Back to have some tallow and beeswax
And a little bread left by workman – a snack!
Take some back for family to eat
In their cosy nest beneath the Vicar's seat!
Now go after Jemima, a wayward mouse
Who's gone searching amidst God's house.
There she is right under the font cover
Take her back to nest and irate mother.

We mice are oft considered a pest
But we keep an eye on the Church – that's best!
Humans say they read the bible every day
Which they follow in ritual to pray and say
They are much like me, the poor church mouse
Who worships diligently each day in God's house!

THE LIGHT OF THE WORLD

T he rising of the sun at dawn
 Brings renewed life and light to our world.
 The sun, a yellow dwarf star,
Leads us in a vain search for
Solitude, solemnity and peace
That influenced Piper to create a magical,
Emotionally charged masterpiece of stained
Glass* of Christ, life giving sun – an
Abstract of 'foliage' cascading in
Brilliant, rich, deep oranges and blues on
Background of shades of acid green and blues.
The sun, Christ incarnate, an intense yellow
Rises and shines to light up our humble earthly life.
It is the Light of the World.
Go in peace.

Main Chapel, Robinson College, Cambridge

ST. ANDREWS, WOODWALTON

ar from anywhere.
Isolated, yet so loved.
The gate lies open.

A chorus of rooks gather noisily
Around the old church tower
But peace reigns in God's Acre
On a glorious, fine, warm late
Summer afternoon overlooking
The chequerboard pattern of
Peaceable, harvest laden Fenland fields.
For a moment the peace is broken
As weary travellers are swept past
In sleek, humming and whirring electric trains.

The church path looks little trodden
Past shoulder high swaying grasses and
Sweet corn in the nearby field.
Bees, birds and insects hum and call
To each other as they garner
Food and harvest for their parlours.
A fox slinks through the drought dried
Long grass as if purposely avoiding
Where many souls rest in peace
Past where owls roost and give thanks
For their food and life
On a rich and heavenly pasture.

Under the ancient porch arch
To enter the cool and evocative
Heart of this rural gem that
Has seen generations of villagers
Pray, be baptised, wedded and carried
Through on their final journey to
Peaceful rest in God's Acre under the
Watchful eye of the church and
Our Guardian and Saviour above.

From the cool peace of St.Andrews' walls
Into the warm, rural tranquillity of
The churchyard as God's bees serenely
Glide from flower to flower.
As the sun shines on their honey making
My time has come to rest
Where, at peace, and the war bravely fought
The Fenman is in his seventh heaven
Close to his beloved Fenland and old railway line!

Enjoy the views.
Rest in peace.
Your work is done.
Sleep your sleep.

THE BEGINNING AND THE END

Vivid and vibrant are the colours that stream
Through the tiny chapel window
At a Cambridge College.*
An evocative vision of Life and the End.
A Romanesque tympanum at Allier
Inspired Piper and Reyntiens
To create stained glass so special –
'The Begininng and the End' – an abstract
Coming together of Adam and Eve, the Last Supper
And the 'End' in vibrant acid green
Whilst above is 'New Life' - Virgin, Child
And the Magi from the same palette –
Rich, deep, fiery blood red colours.
So is the Beginning and the End.
Life is so short upon this earth.
Be at peace.

*Side Chapel at Robinson College, Cambridge

ACKNOWLEDGEMENTS

s always I find it impossible to name everyone who has helped, supported and encouraged me over the time the collection has been in the making. To those who 'chewed the cud' with me over garden and farm gates, in village inns, under lych gates and down country lanes – many thanks and God bless you!

I am most grateful to Robinson College for their kind permission to allow me reproduce 'The Light of the World' [John Piper and Patrick Reyntiens] as Back Cover Illustration and to Steven Cole, photographer, giving permission for the reproduction of 'The Beginning and the End' [John Piper and Patrick Reyntiens] as Front Cover Illustration. Due recognition should be made here to the printers and publishers for their dedicated and hard work. I must also express thanks to my youngest son, David who valiantly assisted me resolve the machinations of the infernal computer which always seemed to have a mind of it's own!

A great debt of gratitude must be expressed to three stalwarts in helping the collection be a success – Charlie Sutton and my eldest son, Christopher, who provided the illustrations - they have my highest and untold appreciation; and the wonderful Chella of Honeybee Books, the publishers, whilst my fantastic friend, Sandra Langwade, based in my home city of Peterborough has guided me in the right direction and persuaded me to pursue 'my dream' of compiling a collection of poems.

Sincere thanks must go to Sophie Foll who acted as PA to the author for assisting and organising marketing and publicity of the book - a valiant task successfully completed.

ABOUT THE AUTHOR

enneth Moore was born in 1947 at Warboys in the then County of Huntingdonshire where many generations of his family worked in the Fens. Brought up for many of his school years in the nearby city of Peterborough including attending the Thomas Deacon Grammar School he then trained as a Chartered Architect in Leicester. He developed his own practice as a specialist in historic and vernacular buildings. He has been deeply involved in the Historic Building Preservation Trust movement for some 20 years being founder and chairman of 3 different trusts.

Some 10 years or so ago he abandoned the drawing board and tee square to concentrate on writing and photography. Some of his articles have been published in specialist and professional magazines. In 2006 he published his first book – *'From Fen to Mountain'* – a travel autobiography that achieved much acclaim. His main hobby is caring for many cacti and succulents whilst also seeking out the unspoilt charm of old English villages and the solitude, solemnity and sanctity of often isolated,rural churches and God's Acre.

He works whilst listening to the relaxing music of Ralph Vaughan Williams, George Butterworth and J S Bach's Organ Concertos, Organ Chorale Preludes and Brandenburg Concertos andTudor Church Music[Richard Dering and Adrian Batten] sung by Peterborough Cathedral Choir directed by Stanley Vann with organist Richard Latham. He likes nothing better but to be present in an ancient and historic cathedral or small rural church and hear the organ playing, hopefully, his favourite chorale preludes and choristers singing Plain Song!

He now lives in Dorset.

ABOUT THE ILLUSTRATORS

Christopher Moore

C hristopher Moore, eldest son of the author was born in the city of Peterborough in 1985 and obtained a BA[Hons] in Fine Art [Valuation] at Southampton. He has written anthropomorphic novels alongside his own sketches and drawings. He now lives in Michigan, USA.

Charlie Sutton

C harlie Sutton was raised in Bridport, Dorset and returned to her home town after graduating with a B.A [Hons] in Illustration from Falmouth University in 2013. She is now a freelance illustrator based in Bridport, Dorset; she can be found designing and painting in her log cabin at the bottom of the garden!

BIBLIOGRAPHY

Almond Philip C. *The Witches of Warboys.* I.B.Tauris[2008]

Mee Arthur. *Bedford and Huntingdon. King's England.*Hodder and Stoughton [1939]

Mee Arthur. *Cambridgeshire. King's England.* Hodder and Stoughton [1949]

Mee Arthur. *Dorset.King's England.* Hodder and Stoughton [1951]

Ordnance Survey. *Landranger Series Maps*

Pevsner Sir Nikolaus. *Bedfordshire,Huntingdon and Peterborough. Buildings of England.* Penguin [1968]

Pevsner Sir Nikolaus. *Cambridgeshire.Buildings of England.* Penguin [1982]

Pevsner Sir Nikolaus. *Dorset. Buildings of England.* Penguin [1972]

Pevsner Sir Nikolaus. *Essex.Buildings of England.*Penguin [1965]

RCHM. *West Dorset.* HMSO [1946]

FORTHCOMING TITLES

By Kenneth Moore

'Strange Tales of the English Countryside' [Short Stories]
'Immortal Fenland Spirits' [Poetry and Verse]
'Sacred and Monastic Havens of Peace and Delight' [Poetry and Verse]